Rivers

of

DIVINE TRUTH

Rivers
of
DIVINE TRUTH

RABBI KIRT A. SCHNEIDER

CHARISMA HOUSE

MOST CHARISMA HOUSE BOOK GROUP products are available at special quantity discounts for bulk purchase for sales promotions, premiums, fund-raising, and educational needs. For details, call us at (407) 333-0600 or visit our website at www.charismahouse.com.

RIVERS OF DIVINE TRUTH by Rabbi Kirt A. Schneider
Published by Charisma House
Charisma Media/Charisma House Book Group
600 Rinehart Road
Lake Mary, Florida 32746

Unless otherwise noted, all Scripture quotations are from the New American Standard Bible, copyright © 1960, 1962, 1963, 1968, 1971, 1972, 1973, 1975, 1977, 1995 by The Lockman Foundation. Used by permission. www.Lockman.org

Scripture quotations marked KJV are from the King James Version of the Bible.

Scripture quotations marked NIV are taken from the Holy Bible, New International Version®, NIV®. Copyright © 1973, 1978, 1984, 2011 by Biblica, Inc.® Used by permission of Zondervan. All rights reserved worldwide. www.zondervan.com. The "NIV" and "New International Version" are trademarks registered in the United States Patent and Trademark Office by Biblica, Inc.®

Scripture quotations marked NKJV are taken from the New King James Version®. Copyright © 1982 by Thomas Nelson. Used by permission. All rights reserved.

Visit the author's website at https://discoveringthejewishjesus.com/.

Library of Congress Cataloging-in-Publication Data:
An application to register this book for cataloging has been
submitted to the Library of Congress.

International Standard Book Number: 978-1-62999-868-8
E-book ISBN: 978-1-62999-869-5

20 21 22 23 24 — 987654321
Printed in the United States of America

Contents

Contents

Acknowledgments

To a degree we are all products of those around us who have invested into our lives. God uses others to impart something of Himself to us. With this in mind, I want to thank my wife, Cynthia, whose nurturing love and wisdom have brought incredible transformation to my soul.

I would also like to thank the *Discovering the Jewish Jesus* staff for their love for HaShem and all the hard work they are doing to advance His kingdom.

And it goes without saying, as always, that most of all, I thank and praise the Lord! Baruch HaShem!

Introduction

Sanctify them in the truth; Your word is truth.

—John 17:17

IN TODAY'S CULTURE truth is relative in the minds of many. Society now believes that truth is defined by the individual. Whether in the political or spiritual realm, instead of being absolute, truth too often is construed as whatever the ever-changing popular consensus is.

But the Bible tells us that truth isn't a matter of opinion. Truth is found in God's Word.

Over the next one hundred days, together we will mine the rivers of truth that flow from the living Word of God. I say *rivers* of truth because God's Word is multifaceted and multidimensional, speaking to every aspect of our lives. Only when we are grounded in the truth are we able to walk in the strength, peace, and victory of God's promises.

There is another reason I refer to *rivers* of truth. Rivers are in motion. This is how God wants our spiritual lives to be. He doesn't want us to be stagnant. He wants us to always be growing in our relationship with Him. His plan is for us to be continuously receiving from the Spirit so that we can continually be changed and transformed into His likeness and so that our doing will be an overflow of our receiving.

The change we desire to see in our lives and world starts with a revelation of truth in our hearts. In Psalm 51:6, David wrote, "Behold, You desire truth in the innermost being, and in the hidden part You will make me know wisdom." God is always more concerned with what is going on inside us than He is with how we appear outwardly. What is inside will eventually come out. Yeshua (Jesus) said, "He who believes in Me, as the Scripture said, 'From his innermost being will flow rivers of living water'" (John 7:38).

My prayer is that as you read these pages you will experience a fresh infilling of God's Word and Spirit, and that as you are filled with more and more of Him, you will share His truth with those around you. A body of water that has no way to flow out will become like a swamp—stagnant, foul, and polluted. But a body of water that has an outflow is going to stay useful and pure. In a similar way, God wants His truth to not only flow into us but to also be released through us, just like a flowing river.

No matter how long we have known the Lord, there is always more. God's wisdom and revelation are constantly being imparted to us as we digest His Word. Yeshua said, "He who eats My flesh and drinks My blood has eternal life" (John 6:54) and "the words that I speak unto you, they are spirit, and they are life" (John 6:63, KJV). We must seize them by going before the Father each day to learn of Him, to grow in His love and truth.

A NOTE ABOUT TERMINOLOGY

You'll find throughout this devotional that I sometimes use the name *Yahweh* when referring to God. This is God's covenant name that He revealed to His people in Exodus 6:3. It is often translated "LORD" in the Old Testament.

Another name that I use for God is HaShem, which is translated in English as "The Name." Within the culture of Judaism there is a sense that God is so holy that His actual name is not pronounced and He is simply referred to as "The Name." Additionally, I sometimes refer to God as *Adonai*, which means "Lord" in Hebrew. It's the name Jewish people use when referring to God in their liturgical prayers.

I also use other Hebrew terms that may already be familiar to you, including *Yeshua* (Jesus), *Ruach HaKodesh* (the Holy Spirit), and *HaMashiach* (the Messiah).

Choose to Be His

I am my beloved's and my beloved is mine.
—Song of Solomon 6:3

THIS VERSE MAY be familiar to you if you've read the Song of Solomon (also called the Song of Songs). The book paints a picture of the relationship we have with our God. As it was with Solomon and his bride, so it is with us: we are God's, and He is ours.

Beloved, you are important to God. He created you and me because He wanted our friendship. James 2:23 tells us that Abraham "was called the friend of God." Can you imagine? God called Abraham His *yedeed* (Hebrew for *friend*). But friendship with God isn't only for Abraham. It is for you and me as well (Gal. 3:14).

Yeshua said, "No longer do I call you slaves, for the slave does not know what his master is doing; but I have called you friends, for all things that I have heard from My Father I have made known to you" (John 15:15). God gets pleasure from being in relationship with us. But as with any good relationship, both sides must choose to value the other.

We exist within God, because everything God created exists within Him. He holds the entire universe together. Yet while we exist within Him, we are separate from Him until we choose to unite with Him. We are unique human beings. The reason God made us independent from Him is because He wanted a real love relationship with us, and the only way that could happen is if we had to choose to love Him. Because we're in Him but unique from Him, we must choose to unite with Him.

I want to ask you a question today: Are you choosing every day to join yourself to God for His pleasure—to be His? When we choose to be His, we wake up in the morning and begin the day by bringing Him into our consciousness. Then we consciously give ourselves to Him by doing things that please Him such as cultivating an awareness of His presence, praying, reaching out to help others, and spending time in the Word. Beloved, we are His. We were created for Him, and when we give ourselves to Him, we fulfill the reason for which He made us—to be joined and united to Him.

Father God, I surrender myself fully to You now. I choose to make myself Yours. Father, I ask that You help me love You and make Your Son the priority of my life.

You Are Beautiful to God

> God created man in His own image, in the image
> of God He created him; male and female He
> created them.
>
> —GENESIS 1:27

WITH ITS GORGEOUS bluish-green color, the Mediterranean Sea, viewed from Caesarea, Israel, is one of the most beautiful sights I've ever seen. And its splendor reminds me of how beautiful God is. Sometimes when we think of God's nature, we think about His holiness, His justice, or His moral attributes. Or we may think about His omnipotence and His omniscience, that He's all-powerful and all-knowing. But when people think of God, they often don't realize that one of His most foundational attributes is His beauty.

The beauty of God is reflected in the world around us. The Bible says in Romans 1:20 that "since the creation of the world His invisible attributes, His eternal power and divine nature, have been clearly seen, being understood through what has been made, so that they are without excuse." In other words, God's attributes are not unknown to us; we can understand much of who He is through what He has made on the earth.

That's what happened to me when I looked at the gorgeous turquoise water of the Mediterranean. It was so remarkable it was almost beyond words, and its beauty gave me a deeper sense of the reality of the beauty of HaShem.

But it isn't only nature that reflects the beauty of God. Beloved, I want to tell you today that because you're made in God's image, you're beautiful too. The devil is called the accuser of the brethren for a reason; he accuses God's people day and night, trying to cover us with dirt and shame. But I want you to know it's all a lie. You're beautiful to God, and He loves you. What is inside you is more beautiful than the Mediterranean Sea.

Father God, You are beautiful, and Your beauty is reflected in what You have made. Lord, help me to ignore the lies of the enemy and believe that because I am made in Your image, I am beautiful too. Father, I ask that You give me a spirit of wisdom and revelation to know You and how You see me.

Live Beyond Your Understanding

Trust in the LORD with all your heart and do not lean on your own understanding.

—PROVERBS 3:5

WHY DOES SOLOMON, the wisest man in the whole world, who wrote today's verse, tell us to trust in the Lord with all our heart and not lean on our own understanding? Because of this reality: "My thoughts are not your thoughts, nor are your ways My ways....For as the heavens are higher than the earth, so are My ways higher than your ways and My thoughts than your thoughts," says the Lord (Isa. 55:8–9).

A lot of times the Lord will lead us to do something that makes no sense. When we feel God's Spirit telling us something that seems to contradict our own understanding, we have to make a decision. Are we going to follow what we believe to be the directive of Yeshua? Or are we going to lean on our own understanding?

Years ago I was on my way somewhere, and I was

taking a route I used to go almost every day. But on this particular day I strongly felt the Lord say, "Don't go that way today. Go this way." It made no sense to me because my normal route was the fastest course. But the impression was so strong in my spirit that I said, "Lord, it seems like I'm clearly hearing Your Spirit telling me to go a different way, but it makes absolutely no sense. So Lord, I'm going to go the way I usually go, but I'm marking this moment because if I go my usual route and something goes wrong, I'll know I was hearing Your voice, and I won't make the same mistake again."

Sure enough, when I didn't heed the voice of the Lord, I ended up in a huge traffic jam. I was clearly hearing the voice of Father God, but I didn't follow it because it went against my own understanding. Beloved, let's be open to the Lord's voice. Let's believe that we really do experience God's leading and choose to yield to and obey Him, because as we do, God is going to lead us into a depth with Him we could never have experienced if we'd lived only by our own understanding.

> *Father God, help me not to cling to my own understanding too tightly. Make clear to me when You're speaking so I can follow Your voice. Help me to grow in trust so I follow You without debate or hesitation.*

DAY 4

Rejoice Continually

For in the day of trouble He will conceal me in His tabernacle; in the secret place of His tent He will hide me; He will lift me up on a rock. And now my head will be lifted up above my enemies around me, and I will offer in His tent sacrifices with shouts of joy; I will sing, yes, I will sing praises to the LORD.
—PSALM 27:5–6

THE LORD RECENTLY spoke to me audibly. I was in my prayer room listening to beautiful worship music, kind of half asleep and half awake. And just as I was fully coming awake, I literally heard the Lord speak in my soul, and this is what He said: "Rejoice continually, and you will overcome every obstacle."

Rejoice continually. This wasn't something I had been thinking about or focusing on intentionally. Rather, it was a word the Lord Himself, who lives inside me, communicated to me through His Spirit.

This message that God spoke to me is what David was articulating in today's passage. God wants us to take hold of that warrior spirit that chooses to praise Him. We don't get to appoint what challenges we face in life, but we can determine how we respond to them. God wants us to choose to rejoice so we can overcome.

The prophet Habakkuk prayed, "Though the fig tree should not blossom and there be no fruit on the vines, though the yield of the olive should fail and the fields produce no food, though the flock should be cut off from the fold and there be no cattle in the stalls, yet I will exult in the Lord, I will rejoice in the God of my salvation" (Hab. 3:17–18).

Habakkuk understood that when we rejoice, our focus moves from our problems and pain to the goodness and greatness of our God. And as we think about His power and majesty, we are reminded that nothing is too hard for Him. As the psalmist proclaimed, "Great is our Lord and abundant in strength; His understanding is infinite. The LORD supports the afflicted" (Ps. 147:5–6). So, beloved, elect to rejoice continually even when your life is hard, because that is how you will overcome every obstacle.

Father, thank You for Your Word. Help me to choose to rejoice, no matter what I face in life. I believe in doing so I will overcome.

Just Ask

> If you then, being evil, know how to give good gifts
> to your children, how much more will your heav-
> enly Father give the Holy Spirit to those who ask
> Him?
>
> —LUKE 11:13

TODAY'S PASSAGE REVEALS three key truths that every follower of Yeshua must know and receive to experience real intimacy with the Father.

First, the fact that Jesus said "you, being evil" when speaking to His followers tells us that even we as believers in Yeshua struggle with evil within us. Paul said, "In my flesh dwelleth no good thing" (Rom. 7:18, KJV). But we also have goodness and beauty in us because we're created in God's image. That's why we see human beings do loving, kind, and compassionate things. Although we still struggle with evil as believers and have to overcome it, we're forgiven and being cleansed through the blood of Yeshua and the working of the Spirit and Word of God.

The second truth we must believe is that God wants to give us good gifts. Earthly parents who love their children want to bless them, and God is no different. Psalm 84:11 says, "No good thing does He withhold from those who walk uprightly." Believe the Father wants to bless you.

This brings us to the third point. Jesus said Father would give good gifts to those who ask. Frequently great things don't just randomly fall on people from above. People often receive God's gifts because they ask. James 4:2 says, "You do not have because you do not ask." So, beloved, ask Him to strengthen you in His peace and love. Ask Him to change your mind when your thoughts are off base. Ask Him to work in your life so you can experience Him in a more real way and enjoy His presence more thoroughly. If you ask Him for anything according to His will, He will do it. The Father gives good gifts to those who ask, and as Yeshua said, everyone who asks receives (Luke 11:10).

Father God, You are a good Father who gives good gifts to Your children. I believe that You answer my prayers, and I love You, Father.

Unshakable Peace

Peace I leave with you; My peace I give to you; not as the world gives do I give to you. Do not let your heart be troubled, nor let it be fearful.

—JOHN 14:27

THERE IS A type of peace the world gives. The problem is that it's a fleeting and superficial peace. When everything is going well—when all the elements of our circumstances are going just right, all our relationships are going smoothly, and everything is good on the surface of our lives—we can feel a sense of peace. But there is a problem, and it is twofold. First, the peace has no depth, and second, it's temporary, because as soon as the circumstances change, that peace will go away.

But the peace God imparts to us is deep, and it's rooted in something unshakeable—God Himself. Yeshua was able to stand before Pilate, who was threatening to crucify Him, completely unshaken because He had God's peace. As His accusers were yelling for Pilate to do away with Him, Jesus was so unmoved by their taunts that it scared them. Why didn't Jesus react?

Because He walked in the very essence of God's peace. God wants to impart this peace to you and me. But we have to make space for Him in our lives to receive it.

Yeshua said, "I stand at the door and knock; if anyone hears My voice and opens the door, I will come in to him and will dine with him, and he with Me" (Rev. 3:20). Beloved, let's open up our souls by putting God first in our lives. Let's honor Him with our hearts' intent and our actions. When we do this, we create a place of habitation within us. When we make Him first in our lives, we create a channel for the Spirit of God to come in and impart His very nature and peace within us.

> *Father God, thank You for Your peace that passes all understanding. I open the door of my heart so You can come in and make my heart Your home. Help me to make You first. My heart's desire is to know You, love You, and experience the reality of Your supernatural peace.*

His Love Can't Be Quenched

> Many waters cannot quench love, nor will rivers
> overflow it; if a man were to give all the riches of
> his house for love, it would be utterly despised.
> —SONG OF SOLOMON 8:7

RECENTLY I VISITED the deep forests of Colorado,
and there were two mighty rivers. Even though they
weren't very wide, the water running through them was
so powerful that if I had stepped into the water, it would
have pushed me over.

The Bible tells us in today's verse that as powerful as
the waters running through those rivers were, even that
strength cannot put out love. In fact, nothing on earth
can quench the power of love. Love is the most powerful
thing in the universe, and it's not even a thing. It's a man-
ifestation. Love is an emanation of God Himself.

The Bible says faith, hope, and love will endure into
eternity, but the most powerful of all is love (1 Cor. 13:13).
Love caused God to send His Son to die for our sins. First
John 4:8 tells us plainly—God is love.

The biggest challenge you and I have is to believe that

Father God really loves us. We can say we believe He loves us, but in truth, we often struggle to fully embrace this reality. We sometimes don't feel worthy. We look at our sin and feel shame, and as a result we don't let love in. But the Bible says, "Behold what manner of love the Father has bestowed on us, that we should be called children of God!" (1 John 3:1, NKJV), and, "But God demonstrates His own love toward us, in that while we were yet sinners, Christ died for us" (Rom. 5:8).

So I want to leave you with two challenges today. First, let's really believe Father loves us and that we could never do anything to stop Him from loving us. There is no condemnation for those who are in Christ Jesus. And second, because God is love, let's practice loving others, not because they deserve it but simply because God is love, and because He loves, we love.

So, beloved, let's expand our hearts and open our minds to believe in our Father's love and let the deep rivers of the Spirit's love in. We're His best, every single one of us. Let's believe that and receive it.

> *Father, help me open my heart and mind to receive Your love. And, Father, I ask that You present opportunities for me to share Your love with others.*

DAY 8

God Is Near

But as for me, the nearness of God is my good; I
have made the Lord God my refuge, that I may tell
of all Your works.

—Psalm 73:28

WHAT A BEAUTIFUL verse. The psalmist declares,
"My portion in life is God's nearness to me." I don't
know about you, but that comforts me. God is near—we
have been given the abiding gift of the Ruach HaKodesh,
the Holy Spirit. God is here (Acts 2)!

God is so near to His children. We see this truth again
and again in the Scriptures. David proclaimed that "the
Lord is near to all who call upon Him, to all who call
upon Him in truth" (Ps. 145:18). Father spoke through
the prophet Jeremiah, saying, "'Am I a God who is near,'
declares the Lord, 'And not a God far off?'" (Jer. 23:23).
God is here wherever we are.

The truth is, however, that sometimes we feel the Lord
is not near. Sometimes, because we're facing a problem
or because of our emotions, we feel that God is far away,
but I want to encourage you to look for Him in your

life. Look for Jesus to manifest Himself in your circumstances. Look for Yeshua to speak to you in your dreams. Look for Him to give you wisdom through another person. Look for Him in divine synchronicities. Trust in the Holy Spirit who bears witness with your spirit.

God is near, but we have to be looking for Him or we'll miss Him. Paul said that God made mankind "that they would seek God, if perhaps they might grope for Him and find Him, though He is not far from each one of us" (Acts 17:27). Beloved, God loves you more than you realize, and He is nearer to you than your own breath. Open your heart. Believe that God loves you, is with you, and will never leave you nor forsake you. Baruch HaShem (Bless the Lord)!

> *Father God, thank You for being near to me. Help me not to miss Your hand at work in my life. Open my eyes to see You revealing Yourself in the situations I face, even through my conversations with others. Give me revelation of Your closeness. Father, Your Word declares that if I seek You, I will find You. As I pursue You, Father, cause me to experience Your presence and receive a deeper revelation of Your love for me.*

He Will Guide You

He guides me in the paths of righteousness for His name's sake.

—Psalm 23:3

IT IS SUCH a comfort to know Father God will lead and guide me. None of us knows the future. We don't know what's going to happen tomorrow. We don't always know if we should choose *A* or *B* because they both look like good options. But Father knows which option is best, because He knows where He wants to take us, and He knows what is going to happen tomorrow. To me, this is such an encouragement. I don't know how I could live without the confidence that Father God will lead and guide me as David says in Psalm 23.

Perhaps you're feeling some anxiety about a future decision you have to make, or maybe you're concerned about whether a decision you recently made was the right one. I want to encourage you to just continue to look to God. As many of you now know, Jews often refer to God as HaShem, a Hebrew term that means "The Name." It's a reminder that God is big—so much bigger than the box we put Him in. He is unlimited and is not confined to time and space; He can even override bad decisions you have made and use them for good.

The Scriptures tell us, "In all your ways acknowledge Him, and He will make your paths straight" (Prov. 3:6). God doesn't just lead us along any path; He leads us in the way we should go—the way that will lead us to the good future God has planned for us. "For I know the thoughts that I think toward you, saith the LORD, thoughts of peace, and not of evil, to give you an expected end" (Jer. 29:11, KJV). God has a destination for each of us, and He knows the path that will get us there.

So be encouraged, beloved. You're not alone in this world. It's not all up to you. As you continue to put your trust in God through Yeshua, He is going to continue to lead and guide you in life.

> *Father God, thank You for leading and guiding me. I don't know the future, and I don't always know which path to take. But You know the plans You have for me and exactly what needs to happen for me to fulfill my destiny. Help me to have confidence in Your love and leading. You are limitless and nothing is too difficult for You!*

The Heart of the Matter

Let the words of my mouth and the meditation of
my heart be acceptable in Your sight, O LORD, my
rock and my Redeemer.

—PSALM 19:14

OFTENTIMES WE ARE mindful of outward sin. We
repent of things that are obvious in the flesh, such
as cursing, sexual immorality, or abusing drugs or alcohol.
This awareness of sin is important, but sometimes once
we address those external issues, we think we're done. We
don't realize that God is just as concerned about cleaning
up the internal issues that separate us from Him.

David's prayer in today's verse wasn't just to be clean
outwardly; he also wanted his words and his thoughts—
the meditations of his heart—to be clean before God.
Father certainly cares about our outward sins, but He has
always been most concerned about what is happening in
our hearts. That is because our hearts reveal who we truly
are. Proverbs 27:19 says, "As in water face reflects face, so
the heart of man reflects man." We may be able to hide
our faults from those around us, but nothing is hidden

from HaShem. The psalmist declared, "Would not God find this out? For He knows the secrets of the heart" (Ps. 44:21).

Beloved, I want to encourage you today: Don't just focus on the outward sin. Ask the Lord to reveal to you what is happening in your heart. Ask Him if the words of your mouth are pleasing to Him. Ask Him if the things you're thinking about are acceptable in His sight. Let's pray for a cleansing of our souls at the deepest level.

If we'll be open and transparent with Him and allow the Ruach HaKodesh, the Spirit of God, to convict us of the words we speak and the things we meditate on that are not in line with HaShem's will, we will be cleansed inside and out as the power of the Holy Spirit washes and regenerates us. As a result of that cleansing, we'll feel closer to Father God and more connected to Jesus.

> *Father, I want the words of my mouth and the meditations of my heart to be acceptable in Your sight. Make me aware of what is truly happening in my heart. I want to be in alignment with You and experience Your peace in my soul.*

DAY 11

You Are His

For my father and my mother have forsaken me,
but the LORD will take me up.

—PSALM 27:10

PSALM 27 WAS written by David, who experienced
rejection because of his love for Yeshua. David knew
Jesus personally, as is referenced in Psalm 110:1 and Matthew 22:41–45.

As a Jewish believer in Yeshua, I can relate to these
words David wrote. When I embraced Yeshua as Messiah,
my parents felt they had to reject that part of me, and
since Yeshua became everything to me, it was as if they
were rejecting me. But Jesus said in the Sermon on the
Mount, "Blessed are you when men hate you, and ostra-
cize you, and insult you, and scorn your name as evil, for
the sake of the Son of Man. Be glad in that day and leap
for joy, for behold, your reward is great in heaven" (Luke
6:22–23).

In today's verse, we see the tenderness of God's relationship with David. Though he had been forsaken by his
family, David knew that he was safe in the arms of his

real and heavenly Father. Beloved, that is the kind of soft, tender relationship you can have with God. No matter who has forsaken you in life, no matter what you've been through in your past, the Lord will take you up. He won't let you irrevocably stumble or fall.

A friend of mine once told me of a season in his life when he was going through a difficult time. He had given away all his money to follow the Lord, and he felt forsaken because he had nothing. But God came to him supernaturally, picked him up, and set him on a journey that led him into ministry. Today, he works with me, touching lives all over the world with the anointing Father has put on his life.

Beloved, when you're forsaken—whether it be by your mother, your father, or a friend—know this: God will always take you up when you're His. HaShem's love for you will never fail.

> *Father, thank You for never leaving me nor forsaking me. Thank You for taking me up and never letting me fall. I am so blessed that You are my true Father forever and that because of You I will not fall. In Messiah Yeshua.*

Make God Your Confidence

Though a host encamp against me, my heart will
not fear; though war arise against me, in spite of
this I shall be confident.

—PSALM 27:3

DAVID IS A primary figure not only within Judaism
but to everyone who believes the Bible. He was
described as a man who was after (in pursuit of) God's
own heart. It is powerful and beautiful that although
he was a warrior, David had a sensitive soul and loved
HaShem deeply. And as today's verse indicates, he had
incredible confidence in God.

Every human being in every generation is assaulted by
fear at some point. All around us there are problems and
threats that we can neither prevent nor control. Natural
disasters sometimes strike without warning. An accident or bad doctor's report can change a person's life in
a moment. Financial concerns torment many. And, of
course, the biggest fear that plagues mankind is the fear
of death. Why? Because we have no control over it. We
don't know when or how we're going to die, and sadly,

many people have no idea where they're going when they die, and the fear of the unknown is the most ominous of all.

But when we put our confidence in God, no matter what we're facing—whether it's death, things past, things present, things to come, or any created thing—we become more than conquerors through Him who loves us. (See Romans 8:35–39.) God is our confidence. David declared, "The LORD is my light and my salvation; whom shall I fear? The LORD is the defense of my life; whom shall I dread?" (Ps. 27:1). I believe Messiah Jesus is saying to you and me today, "Be strong and courageous in Me. Be afraid of nothing."

> *Father, Your Word tells us over a hundred times not to be afraid; forgive me for fearing. I ask You to help me walk in divine courage. In this life, I'm surrounded by so many circumstances that seek to put fear and dread on me. Father God, I ask You to strengthen my confidence in You today. Father, by the power of the Ruach HaKodesh, deepen my intimacy with You so I will have the confidence in You that David expressed in Psalm 27 and I won't fear anything or anyone. I ask this in Yeshua's name.*

The Breath of God

Then the LORD God formed man of dust from the ground, and breathed into his nostrils the breath of life; and man became a living being.

—GENESIS 2:7

TODAY'S VERSE REVEALS a simple but profound truth: *God created you.* You are more than the result of a cosmic, random explosion that happened millions of years ago. You were made on purpose for a purpose. God created you and me, and He placed His divine blueprint and His life inside us. How do we know that? The Book of Genesis tells us that Yahweh Elohim, the Lord God, the Creator of the universe, made us in His own image and breathed His life into us.

The apostle Paul prayed that God's people would know "what are the riches of the glory of His inheritance *in the saints*" (Eph. 1:18, emphasis added). Beloved, there is something in you that is so sacred, so special, so rich, and so much bigger than your human flesh. Your physical body doesn't even begin to manifest the reality of who you are. What's inside you is so much greater and more beautiful than your physical self.

If we live long enough, our bodies are going to begin to degenerate and eventually wear out. But our bodies are not who we are. God breathed His very life into us. He created us with an immortal soul that has His imprint in it, and beyond this, those of us who have received Jesus have been given the gift of the Ruach HaKodesh. God's Spirit now literally lives inside us, and we are partakers of His divine nature.

Eye has not seen and ear has not heard, neither has it ever entered into the heart of man the things that God has prepared for those who love Him (1 Cor. 2:9). Beloved, let's stay focused on HaShem and who we are in Him. No one can define you but God. You are His child, and God's Spirit, not a cosmic accident, is the source of and reason for your life.

Father God, I know my life is not an accident. I was made in Your image, and Your life flows through me. You made me fearfully and wonderfully. I pray that the eyes of my heart will be enlightened, so I will know what is the hope of Your calling and the riches of the glory of Your inheritance in me, Your child. Father, help me to know how precious I am to You and to live out the purpose for which I was created. In Yeshua's name, amen.

Get Still Before God

Be still, and know that I am God.

—PSALM 46:10, NKJV

HAVE YOU EVER sought to be still before the Lord? If not, this is a discipline I encourage you to create. Even if you begin with just fifteen or thirty minutes a day, quiet your heart before the Lord. On a daily basis, just sit before Him. Listen to gentle worship music. I love to go to the prayer room at IHOPKC.org, the International House of Prayer in Kansas City, Missouri, and livestream worship music that puts my focus on the Lord and not on my situation, needs, or problems. As the worship music ascends vertically to HaShem and the words of Scripture are sung, I just sit there before the Lord to receive His presence.

Beloved, when we are still before the Lord, He imparts Himself to us. In 1 Kings 19:11–13, the Lord told the prophet Elijah in essence, "I'm not in the wind; I'm not in the earthquake; I'm not in the fire. I'm in the still, small voice." Oftentimes we don't have the discernment to recognize the gentle promptings of the Ruach HaKodesh, the Holy Spirit, until we've stilled our hearts before Him. Paul said, "Discipline yourself for the purpose of godliness" (1 Tim. 4:7). It takes discipline, willpower, determination, and commitment to create a daily time to just sit before the Lord in stillness. And remember that "He is a rewarder of those who diligently seek Him" (Heb. 11:6, NKJV).

The Lord flat-out tells us in Psalm 46:10 to "be still, and know that I am God" (NKJV). This means there is something we must do to cooperate with God. He told us to be still—turn off the phone, turn off the television, turn off the distractions and the noise, and just settle before the Lord. You may want to listen to gentle worship music, as I often do. As you practice God's presence by stilling your heart, the Holy Spirit will tenderize your heart so you can better discern His leading in your life. We must practice pulling ourselves out of the material world so we can learn to live from the inside out.

Father, help me to prioritize spending time with You, getting quiet before You each day to worship You and listen for Your voice. I want to be led by Your Spirit. As I get still before You each day, Lord, train me to discern Your Spirit's leading.

Get Your Breakthrough

And it shall come to pass in that day, that his
burden shall be taken away from off thy shoulder,
and his yoke from off thy neck, and the yoke shall
be destroyed because of the anointing.
—ISAIAH 10:27, KJV

WHEN GOD'S ANOINTING upon us reaches a certain level of strength, it results in breakthrough.
It becomes a breaker anointing, a type of spiritual
power that arises within us in violence against the devil
and his schemes. Jesus used force to drive out demons,
raise Lazarus from the dead, and overthrow the money
changers in the temple. This paints a picture of the breaker
anointing. To get free of the demonic forces that torment
us and our loved ones, we have to turn on the oppressor—
so that the very thing that was hunting us down becomes
the hunted. We need to go from being a victim to arising,
breaking out, and becoming the victor—turning on Satan
and the powers of darkness.

Remember, when we receive Jesus, we take on His likeness. First John 3:8 says, "The Son of God appeared for this

purpose, to destroy the works of the devil." The breaker anointing will manifest when the anointing of Yeshua so takes possession of us that we naturally rise up to turn on the devil and exercise authority over the powers of darkness. This anointing will shatter the enemy's works, remove hindrances, and create a forward path!

God wants our lives to reflect Him. We must have a "not-to-be-denied" mindset like Jacob had when he took hold of the angel and said to the Lord, "I am not going to let go until you bless me." (See Genesis 32:22–31.) Beloved, breakthrough requires that you have this same winning spirit, which says, "I will have a breaker anointing, and I will pursue God until it is mine!"

When you set your intention on an all-out pursuit of God, you are going to get strong! When you get strong, you will be happy. You are going to enter into this breaker anointing realm. If you do not give up, you will get your breakthrough!

> *Father God, I will not rest until all Your promises of freedom and breakthrough are fulfilled in my life. My Messiah Jesus said, "If the Son sets you free, you will be free indeed." Like Jacob, I will not let go until You bless me. I will walk in the breaker anointing, in Yeshua's name.*

DAY 16

Be Led by the Spirit

But when He, the Spirit of truth, comes, He will guide you into all the truth; for He will not speak on His own initiative, but whatever He hears, He will speak.

—JOHN 16:13

THE SPIRIT OF the Lord was with the children of Israel in the wilderness when they were living in tents around the tabernacle, called in Hebrew the *mishkan*. By night the Holy Spirit manifested over the tabernacle as a pillar of fire. During the day, the Spirit of God, or Ruach HaKodesh, took the form of a glory cloud.

The Bible tells us in Numbers 9 that when the Spirit of the Lord stopped, either in the form of fire or a cloud, the children of Israel would stop and camp there. But whenever the Spirit of the Lord lifted, when either the fire or the glory cloud began to move, they would take up camp and follow the Spirit wherever He led. The Israelites never knew when the cloud or fire was going to move. Sometimes it was two days, sometimes two months, or sometimes even two years. They had to keep their eyes on God's Spirit, follow, and obey.

Beloved, think about it. If the divine fire or the cloud were stationary over the tabernacle, but the Israelites got antsy and decided on their own to move, what would have happened? They would have died in the wilderness and fallen short of the Promised Land because there would have been no provision, protection, or direction for them. Conversely, what would have happened if the Spirit of the Lord had moved and they said, "We're comfortable here; we're not going to move"? They also would have died in the wilderness, because there would have been no food and water, safeguard, or guidance there from God. Not only that, they would have missed their destiny!

It is the same for us today. God still desires to direct our path. Instead of leading us by a fire or a cloud, He has placed His Spirit inside us. But are we following? Are we paying attention to the inner witness of the Holy Spirit who is leading us? If we want to enter into God's fullness in our lives, we must follow the Holy Spirit's lead—moving where and when He directs us. And conversely, we must stop running ahead of Him when He is not authorizing us to go.

Father God, teach and train me to obey and be led by Your Spirit within me. I want to hear Your voice and discern Your direction.

Yeshua's Blood Is Our Confidence

Therefore, brethren, since we have confidence to enter the holy place by the blood of Jesus…let us draw near with a sincere heart in full assurance of faith, having our hearts sprinkled clean from an evil conscience and our bodies washed with pure water.

—HEBREWS 10:19, 22

BELOVED, JESUS DIED for your sins. Because of that one thing, because of what He has done, you can go before the Father every single day, confident in His love for you. I know how convincing the enemy's lies can sound. But every time he tells you God is angry with you or that you're not worthy, remind yourself that the blood of Jesus makes you worthy, not your own goodness.

God loves you right where you are. He loves you too much to leave you there, but He loves you just as you are, and that will never change. So be confident in God's love for you and know that you can go boldly before Him because Jesus' blood has made you clean.

Oftentimes we let the devil keep us from having the confidence to go before God because he accuses us of our sin, and as a result we feel shame and unworthy of HaShem's love and blessing. We know we're not perfect and feel that we've somehow let Father down and don't deserve His goodness. But the author of the Book of Hebrews tells us that we should have confidence in His love for us and our place in His heart.

If our right standing before God could have been based on our own works, Jesus never would have had to come to earth and die for us. But because God knew we could never be made righteous through our own efforts, He sent Yeshua to die for our sins. Because of Jesus, we can come boldly before the throne of grace to obtain help from HaShem.

Yeshua, not our own goodness, is the source of our confidence! Amen?

Father God, because of Yeshua, I come boldly before You, and I believe that Yeshua's blood has washed me clean. I will draw near to You and not shrink back. I am confident in Your love for me and in what Jesus' blood accomplished for me on the cross.

The God of the Now

> I would have despaired unless I had believed that
> I would see the goodness of the LORD in the land
> of the living.
>
> —PSALM 27:13

IN 1978 WHEN Jesus supernaturally manifested Himself
to me in my bedroom in a suburb of Cleveland, Ohio, I
instantly became aware of the fact that God was real, that
He was alive, and that Yeshua was the way to Him. And
ever since that time, my heart's desire has been to experience the presence of God in my life. I'm not just waiting
to die and go to heaven; I want to experience more of God
here on earth.

Sometimes people hear a gospel preached that goes
something like this: "If you receive Jesus, you'll be saved
from your sins, and when you die, you'll go to heaven." So
people go to the altar, repeat a prayer someone told them
to say, and leave after being told their sins are forgiven.
Then they pretty much think all there is for the rest of
their Christian life is to study the Bible and wait to die
and go to heaven.

But in today's verse, David says he would have despaired if he hadn't believed he would see the Lord right now while he was still in the land of the living. David expected to experience God's presence in his lifetime. He believed he could see God's beauty, power, love, compassion, and glory on this side of eternity. And David said in essence, "If I didn't believe that, I would have no reason for living. I'd be in despair just to wake up every day." David's passion was God Himself. He said, "One thing do I seek—to be in Your temple all the days of my life and experience Your beauty." (See Psalm 27:4.)

So my prayer, beloved one, is that you and I will understand as David did that we can experience God today, because HaShem is not only our God forever after; He's the God of the now.

Father God, like David I cry out to experience Your presence in the land of the living. I pray for more of You—more of Your presence and power, more of Your glory and beauty on this side of eternity. Thank You, Father God, for revealing Yourself to me today and continuously in a brand-new way.

DAY 19

Just a Hint

And I heard a loud voice from the throne, saying,
"Behold, the tabernacle of God is among men, and
He will dwell among them, and they shall be His
people, and God Himself will be among them."

—REVELATION 21:3

As YOU MAY know, I enjoy spending time in nature.
The beauty of God's creation can be breathtaking.
When you see the majestic forests, the deer, the foxes,
the hummingbirds, and the awe-inspiring mountains,
it is so evident that there is an incredible, intelligent
Creator who designed everything that exists. But can
you even begin to imagine how beautiful it's going to
be when the tabernacle of God is among men and we
see Him face to face in heaven?

Today's verse tells us that in the new heaven and
the new earth, Adonai will literally dwell among us.
The Bible also says in 1 John 3:2 that when Yeshua
appears, we're going to see Him as He is. Everything
we see is going to be pulsating with life—the plants,
flowers, music, and the river of life. It is going to be

indescribable. First Corinthians 2:9 says, "Eye has not seen and ear has not heard, and which have not entered the heart of man, all that God has prepared for those who love Him."

Beloved, the beauty we see now in nature is just a hint of the glory your heavenly Father has prepared for you. Some of us have forgotten that this world is not our home. We are only passing through here. We are citizens of heaven (Phil. 3:20–21). So let's be encouraged today. Give Him thanks, have hope, and know that we have a destiny and a future that will be filled with the inexpressible glory and beauty of God. "Look up and lift up your heads for your redemption draweth nigh" (Luke 21:28, KJV).

Thank You, Father, for choosing mankind to be in relationship with You. Thank You for choosing me. Thank You for writing my name in the Lamb's Book of Life. I love You and through Your power will live for You with a joyful heart today.

He Is Your Hiding Place

You are my hiding place; You preserve me from trouble.

—PSALM 32:7

YEARS AGO, THERE was a popular worship song that you may remember titled "You Are My Hiding Place." The lyrics echo the words in today's verse, and the song is powerful.

We can't know HaShem as our "hiding place" unless we come to a place of dependency, weakness, and humility. The psalmist knew that. He wrote from a place of trust, clinging, and dependency, "You preserve me from trouble." When we realize our need for God's protection and covering, we recognize that He is our only hiding place and that we can abide under the shadow of His wings, under the shelter of His protection. When we walk in this reality, we feel safe and secure, just like the psalmist.

The truth is, we are vulnerable in this world outside of God. So many things are out of our control. At any moment, we could get struck by lightning, killed in a car accident, or diagnosed with a deadly disease. It's only because the Lord is our hiding place that our life is preserved in such a dangerous existence.

Obviously, this doesn't mean we'll never have any challenges, but I don't think any of us has any idea how many troubles God has already protected us from and preserved us in. God loves you today. You can lay your head down on your pillow at night knowing that Father God truly is and will be your hiding place. As Psalm 91 says, "He who dwells in the shelter of the Most High will abide in the shadow of the Almighty. I will say to the Lord, 'My refuge and my fortress, my God, in whom I trust!' For it is He who delivers you from the snare of the trapper and from the deadly pestilence" (vv. 1–3).

> *Father God, thank You for being my hiding place and preserving me from trouble. I know in this world there will be challenges, but I will rejoice because You have overcome the world. I don't know what will happen in the future, but I am trusting today that I am and will always be safe inside You. Help me to live in a place of humility and dependence on You. Father, cause me to experience security and peace in Jesus' name.*

DAY 21

Sow to the Spirit

For the mind set on the flesh is death, but the mind set on the Spirit is life and peace.

—ROMANS 8:6

THE APOSTLE PAUL wrote in Romans 6:23 that "the wages of sin is death," and in Galatians 6:8, "The one who sows to his own flesh will from the flesh reap corruption, but the one who sows to the Spirit will from the Spirit reap eternal life."

In the age we're living in, many are accustomed to doing what gives them instant gratification. But if we sow to the flesh and pursue the things that give us immediate satisfaction, we're going to end up dying for it and reaping destruction. You see, God's way is harder than the devil's way. Living above the lust of the flesh takes discipline and power. We have to think long-term, because if we don't, we'll find ourselves doing things impulsively that make us feel good for an instant but leave us with nothing but emptiness and sorrow.

Think of all the lives that have been ruined because the person did something they thought would make them feel good, but the action brought destruction into their life. It may have been engaging in sexual sin, abusing drugs or alcohol, or losing their temper. Afterward, what is left is remorse, brokenness, and oftentimes even a wasteland of a life. On the other hand, if we discipline our hearts by the Word of God and use the discernment the Holy Spirit gives us to live above the lust of the flesh and the impulses of the soul, we'll get stronger in Yeshua and become healthier. We will reap life and peace, and so many more people will be blessed by our lives.

Beloved, I want to encourage you to follow Adonai God has great plans for you. You're being changed from glory to glory (2 Cor. 3:18) as you sow to the Spirit and not to the flesh.

> *Father God, help me to think long-term, doing the things that please You and not giving in to gratifying my flesh. I know that when I set my mind on the things of the Spirit, I reap life and peace. But if I set my mind on the lust of my flesh, I will reap destruction. Thank You, Father, for having good plans for my life. Strengthen me to follow You so I can enter into and experience Your abundance and all the good things You have in store for me in life.*

Let Him Bring It Into the Light

Search me, O God, and know my heart; try me and know my anxious thoughts; and see if there be any hurtful way in me, and lead me in the everlasting way.

—PSALM 139:23–24

AFTER ADAM AND Eve sinned against God in the garden, they ran and hid from Him. Sometimes in our fallen human nature we do the same thing. But the psalmist's words in today's verse teach us to do the opposite. He trusted in HaShem's love for him and put himself in a position of humility and said to the Lord, "I don't know myself, but You do. Search me and know me. Let me know if there's any impure way in me." Instead of running, the psalmist put himself in the light of God's presence and said, "Lord, if there's something wrong in me, show me what it is because I want to live a pure life before You. Forgive me and cleanse me."

I wonder, Are you and I doing that in our lives? We

don't have to be afraid of God because He already knows everything about us. He already knows what's going on in our lives, and He wants to deliver us. But for that to happen, we need to allow Him to bring into the light those things in our soul or in our thoughts that may be hiding in the darkness.

I don't know about you, but sometimes I find that I have a bad attitude, and I don't know why. So I say, "Lord, I don't know what the root of this is. I don't know why I have this negative attitude. But Father, I ask You to root it out of me. Try me, test me, and purify me. And whatever is at the root of this thing, Father, I ask You to wash me of it by Your Spirit and Word through the blood of Messiah Jesus." Only when we invite Him in to bring what's hidden in our hearts into the light will we be healed. Whatever comes into the light becomes light.

Beloved, don't be like a cockroach that hides in the darkness. Have confidence in God's great love for you. Open up to Him, and let Him transform you by His Word.

Father God, search my heart and know me. Expose anything in my heart that is not like You and cleanse me through the blood of Jesus. I want my life to be pleasing to You, so root out anything in me that is not clear and clean like You. Lead me in Your ways of truth.

Faith Goes Beyond Feeling

Even though I walk through the valley of the shadow of death, I fear no evil, for You are with me; Your rod and Your staff, they comfort me.

—PSALM 23:4

SOMETIMES I FEEL like God is far away because I don't sense His presence. There are times when I'm trying to get hold of God, but I don't feel Him. I don't hear His voice. I go through times—it may be a day, several days, or even longer—when I just feel like He's not communicating with me. But during those seasons, I practice walking by faith rather than my feelings, and I declare that He is with me even when I feel nothing.

This is what David demonstrated in today's verse. You don't necessarily feel God's presence when you're walking through the valley of the shadow of death. But faith goes beyond feeling, and it's rooted and centered in the living Word of God.

David said, "Even though right now I'm walking through this valley, this shadow, this wasteland, this emptiness, where it seems like there's no life, I will fear no evil for You are with me." The same is true for you and me. God is with us wherever we are. He wants to increase our faith by putting us in situations where it appears as though He's not there. He has purposed to bring us to a place where, because of our faith in His Word, we can affirm in our hearts, minds, and emotions that HaShem is with us, though we feel nothing.

Beloved, the truth is that to get to the next level in our spiritual walk, our faith is going to have to be tested. That means we'll have to learn to walk by faith through some valleys of the shadow of death, trusting and affirming God's Word over our lives and circumstances.

God is with you wherever you are today. Affirm that truth and let it take root in your heart. As you do, you will become stronger and stronger.

> *Father God, I declare that even when I walk through the valley of the shadow of death— when I feel like You're far away—I will not fear because I know You are with me. Lord, help me not to be led by my feelings but to be led by Your Spirit. Help me to trust You. Even when I don't feel You, I will trust Your Word, which says You'll never leave me nor forsake me.*

Destined for Victory

You surround me with songs of deliverance. Selah.
—PSALM 32:7

SELAH IS A Hebrew word that means pause. I want you to pause today and meditate on this: The Lord is going to bring deliverance into your life. He is going to cause you to overcome every single obstacle that you face in this world. As you rejoice continually, you will overcome every obstacle!

The Bible tells us that we're more than conquerors through Him who loved us—"that neither death, nor life, nor angels, nor principalities, nor things present, nor things to come, nor powers, nor height, nor depth, nor any other created thing, will be able to separate us from the love of God, which is in Christ Jesus our Lord" (Rom. 8:37–39).

So I want to encourage you to press on. It may be hard. It may seem as if you've been stuck in this place for a long time. Maybe it has been years. But I want you to know that if you cling to God, He is going to sing a song of deliverance over your life, and you will experience His victory. How do I know that? First John 5:4 says he that is born of God overcomes the world.

Beloved, nothing can separate you from the love of God. You are destined for victory. When it's all said and done, His song of deliverance is going to be the identifying characteristic of your life.

> *Father God, I declare the truth of Your Word today, that if You are for me, it doesn't matter who or what is against me. Nothing can separate me from Your love—not "tribulation, or distress, or persecution, or famine, or nakedness, or peril, or sword" (Rom. 8:35). I am more than a conqueror through You, Father, because You love me. I thank You, Father, that "neither death, nor life, nor angels, nor principalities, nor things present, nor things to come, nor powers, nor height, nor depth, nor any other created thing" (Rom. 8:38–39) will ever be able to separate me from Your love. Your Spirit in me has overcome the world, and Your steadfast love for me will never cease!*

Let Him Restore You

The LORD is my shepherd, I shall not want. He makes me lie down in green pastures; He leads me beside quiet waters. He restores my soul.

—PSALM 23:1–3

BELOVED, WE NEED to take time to just be alone with God like David did. The Lord told us through Isaiah, "In repentance and rest you will be saved, in quietness and trust is your strength" (Isa. 30:15). At times we need to break away from all the busyness of life and simply go into nature. God uses those times to impart Himself to us and restore our souls.

I know it's not always easy to get away from all the things that we're used to doing. We're in such a habit of being busy that it's hard to stop that cycle, sit before the Lord, and receive from Him. But there's such a blessing in taking the time to just be quiet and rest in the Lord. So I want to encourage you today to make time in your life to simply sit with the Lord in nature. Look for a quiet place where you can just sit among the trees and listen to the birds. If you live in a cold climate, perhaps you can just look out at the snow blanketing the ground. If you live near the beach, perhaps you can sit and listen to the waves crashing against the shore or take walks on a path through the woods. Just being in the stillness of God's creation reprograms and recalibrates our system to function in such a way that we can receive more of God's presence into our souls.

There have been times in my life when I have felt so tired spiritually that I'd go out into nature and just lie on the ground and ask the Father to restore my soul. Maybe you can relate. Perhaps you feel like I do at times—exhausted. And it's not even just a physical exhaustion; it's a spiritual and emotional exhaustion. But the Lord can restore your soul. If you can find a way to be outside, sit alone with God, and pray to Him from your heart, He will impart renewal and healing by His Spirit. It may not happen all at once, but He is faithful. As you reach out to Him, He will draw near to you and breathe restoration into your soul.

> *Father God, restore my soul. You know how exhausted I feel in my spirit sometimes. Natural sleep isn't even enough. I need You to restore my soul. So, Abba, as I bask in Your beautiful creation, I ask You to impart Your essence and nature to me, in the name of Yeshua.*

DAY 26

Because of His Love

> Now during the day He was teaching in the temple, but at evening He would go out and spend the night on the mount that is called Olivet. And all the people would get up early in the morning to come to Him in the temple to listen to Him.
>
> —LUKE 21:37–38

RECENTLY DURING A trip to Jerusalem, I visited the Southern Steps, which led into the ancient temple. Those were the steps the common person would travel to present a sacrifice, but they also were often referred to as the Teaching Steps because rabbis went to that location to teach their disciples. Many scholars believe Peter also preached his cutting sermon in Acts 2 from this very spot.

Yeshua also taught some of His parables from those steps. Each day, crowds gathered around Him, calling Him Rabbi. He was clothed in the rabbinic anointing, yet He was superior to any of the other leading Jewish figures of His day. In fact, when people heard Him teach, they said, "This man teaches not as our scribes. He teaches as one with authority." (See Mark 1:22.) The anointing on Yeshua HaMashiach was so powerful, the people were astounded.

Beloved, our faith is not rooted in the clouds somewhere. Our faith is rooted in the fact that the transcendent God—the God of eternity, the God who has no beginning and has no end —descended into time and space. Because He loves us so much, He clothed Himself with flesh and blood, lived as a Jew, and ministered right here on the earth from these Southern Steps to the temple.

God is nearer to us than we know. Jesus is present. Even as He incarnated Himself in flesh and blood and walked the Teaching Steps, Yeshua is personally with you right now, touching you by His Spirit, training and teaching you today.

Let's stop just thinking about God in general terms and instead bring Him into the details of our lives. He is not just the God who is "out there." He is the God who became one with you through Messiah Yeshua. He is here and now.

> *Father, thank You for knowing and loving me, specifically, individually, and personally. Thank You for being right here with me in the very details of my life, even knowing the very number of hairs on my head.*

DAY 27

Tell of the Decree of the Lord

I will surely tell of the decree of the LORD: He said
to Me, "You are My Son, today I have begotten You."
—PSALM 2:7

PSALM 2 IS a Messianic psalm that gives us sight into
both David's (the psalm's author) and Messiah Jesus'
heart. And what do we see? The resolve to "tell of the
decree of the LORD"—to be bold witnesses for HaShem
in the earth.

Psalm 19 tells us that the heavens and earth declare the
glory of God, that they give forth speech. What words are
they declaring? The stars above, the moon, the sun, and
the seas—they're all screaming out, "God is glorious! God
is beautiful! God is alive and He is wonderful and good!"

You and I have been created to make His decrees
known in the world as well. There's no such thing as a
silent believer, because when someone is passionately in
love with God, His praise is going to just come out of
their life as if by osmosis. They won't be able to stop it
because it's naturally who they are.

Don't let the enemy hold you back. Paul said, "For

God has not given us a spirit of timidity, but of power and love and discipline. Therefore do not be ashamed of the testimony of our Lord" (2 Tim. 1:7–8). Wherever you go, wherever you are, let the praise of God radiate through your life. Don't be afraid to say, "Praise the Lord" in public. Don't be afraid to speak of Jesus or to give Him thanks openly.

Beloved, we are God's witnesses on the earth. Let's be like the psalmist in Psalm 2 and be beacons of light in the world. We were not meant to hide the gospel under a bushel somewhere. Jesus said, "I put you here to be lights in the earth. I put you on the hill so people can see your light." Let's speak of God's goodness and not be afraid. Let's not allow what anyone thinks stop us from letting others know about the goodness of God. Keep declaring His Word in the earth. Be strong and courageous. Don't be afraid of rejection, and don't let the enemy shut you down.

> *Father God, help me to shine bright in the earth. Let my life declare Your goodness. I will not be shy about praising You openly and giving You thanks in public. I will speak of Your goodness without fear.*

DAY 28

Put Others First

Do nothing from selfishness or empty conceit, but with humility of mind regard one another as more important than yourselves.

—PHILIPPIANS 2:3

THIS IS A really challenging word because the flesh is naturally selfish. That's true for me, and it's true for you.

To give you an example, consider this question. When you get hungry, do you eat for somebody else or for yourself? You eat for yourself. When you sleep, do you sleep for somebody else or for yourself? You see, by nature, the flesh is selfish; it seeks to provide for its own needs. And while on the earth we will always have an animal or fleshly nature. It is part of our makeup. This is true of all of us, but God is asking us to transcend the power of the flesh and our own naturally selfish disposition and practice serving other people, even though it might not feel good to us. Let's remember, however, that just because it doesn't feel good to us doesn't mean it's not the right thing to do.

Philippians 2:4 tells us to not look out only for our own interests but to consider the interests of others (NIV). God is calling us to operate at a higher level. So let's step out of being selfish. Yes, we have to take care of ourselves, but let's live for a greater purpose and put other people's interests above our own when called to do so. Let's bless and serve people. Let's sow into others' lives. Let's go out of our way to speak to them in a way that will strengthen them. Let's show them God's love by doing little acts of kindness in His name. By doing these things, Messiah Jesus said you'll be growing in His grace and be fruitful for His kingdom. The challenge I want to leave with you today is to practice putting other people first.

> *Father God, help me to lay aside selfishness and consider the needs of others. Push me out of my comfort zone to do what is right, whether it feels good to me or not. Give me the grace and the opportunities to serve others and make Your love and goodness known to them. Help me to look beyond my own wants and needs to see the hurt and pain in people's lives. I ask, Yeshua, that You help me to be Your hands and feet in the earth.*

He Knows You

The LORD is good, a stronghold in the day of trouble,
and He knows those who take refuge in Him.
—NAHUM 1:7

FATHER GOD IS omniscient; He knows everybody. But I'm not talking about Him knowing us in the objective sense. I'm talking about Him knowing us intimately and tenderly. He resists the proud, but He knows everyone who seeks to take refuge in Him with a sincere and humble heart.

When we come to Abba as a child, He stoops down because He is tender and sensitive. When we come to Him to take refuge in Him, He meets us in that place. He knows us. The Lord is looking to and fro across the earth for someone who will come to Him and truly rely on Him to be their God.

As you and I come to the Lord with our weaknesses, with our problems, with our needs, with our sin, with our fears and everything else that concerns us, and we open our souls to Him, looking to Him to be our help, He is eager to be our Helper. You can be assured not just that

He knows who you are in a general sense, but that He loves you deeply, personally, and specifically—Jesus said, in fact, God knows every hair on your head (Luke 12:7).

Beloved, God is calling you to take refuge in Him—to talk to Him as you would talk to a friend, to share the deepest needs and burdens of your heart with Him. As you do, be assured that He hears you, knows you, and loves you with the type of tender love a mother and father have for their little child. And He will draw near to you, strengthen you, and be your stronghold in the day of trouble.

Father God, I come to You humbly, seeking refuge in You. You love me so much that You have numbered every hair on my head. Thank You for being concerned about everything in my life. So, Father, I cast all my cares on You because You care for me. You are my Helper, and I will not be afraid. If You are for me, who can be against me? I will be confident in You and in my relationship with You.

DAY 30

One Thing

One thing I have asked from the LORD, that I shall
seek: That I may dwell in the house of the LORD
all the days of my life, to behold the beauty of the
LORD and to meditate in His temple.

—PSALM 27:4

THIS VERSE IS one of my favorite scriptures in the Bible.
David makes it clear that there is one thing each of us
should seek above everything else. Then he tells us what
that one thing is—to dwell in God's presence and experience His beauty all the days of our lives.

David, the king of Israel who would become known as
Israel's greatest leader, wanted above all else to continually experience God's presence. He was saying in essence,
"I can live without everything else. I just want this one
thing from You—that I might dwell in Your house and
in Your presence all the days of my life." With all David
experienced, all the victories he had won and all the
accolades showered on him, more than anything else, he
craved God's presence in his life.

And for David, God's presence was manifest in beauty.

Who is God? He is beauty. Look at creation—the beautiful skies, flowers, rainbows, fish, animals, waterfalls, rivers, and trees. Paul said in Romans 1:20 that we can learn who God is by looking at His creation: "For since the creation of the world His invisible attributes, His eternal power and divine nature, have been clearly seen, being understood through what has been made." The birds, oceans, mountains, sunsets, and butterflies are all imparting to us a sense of how beautiful our God is.

God's presence satisfies. Jesus said, "I am the bread of life; he who comes to Me will not hunger, and he who believes in Me will never thirst" (John 6:35). Let's keep seeking HaShem. Let's keep cultivating a passion for Yahweh and His beauty.

> *Father, may my desire for You exceed all other passions in my life. Your Word says You are a rewarder of those who diligently seek You* (Heb. 11:6) *and that those who seek You find You when they search for You with all their hearts* (Jer. 29:13). *Father, I choose to diligently pursue Your beauty and Your presence. "They who seek the LORD shall not be in want of any good thing"* (Ps. 34:10).

Rivers of Living Water

He who believes in Me, as the Scripture said, "From
his innermost being will flow rivers of living water."
—JOHN 7:38

THERE ARE MANY things that motivate people to follow
Yeshua, but this is what moves me. I'm not after religion; I'm after the reality described in today's verse. I want
rivers of living water to flow from my innermost being.

I like to think of the words Jesus spoke in John 7:38 as
a scientific reality. By depending on Yeshua, we can drink
of the invisible, supernatural waters of His Spirit. The visible world is not ultimately what is real. The visible world
will pass away. What is real is the invisible world that created this visible world. "By faith we understand that the
worlds were prepared by the word of God, so that what is
seen was not made out of things which are visible" (Heb.
11:3). Today's verse is speaking about the scientific reality
of the invisible world that you and I can experience in the
here and now.

Jesus said, "He who believes in Me…." To believe
means more than just saying, "Yes, I believe." It means

we stake our life in what we claim to believe. It means we are so convinced that we live for it. When I survey my life over the last fifteen years, the transformation has been clearly and truly supernatural. People who knew me years ago say, "Rabbi, you're not the same person. Your voice doesn't even sound the same anymore." What is the difference? It's that more and more I've been able to drink from the waters of life.

Beloved, whatever it costs, whatever you have to give up, whatever you have to sacrifice to follow Jesus—do it. Seek Him. Put Him first, and you will drink more and more from these rivers of living water that Jesus promised. More and more you will live from the inside out rather than from the outside in, and a well of living water will spring up from the inside of you. Living waters will flow forth from you, changing both your life and those around you.

> *Father God, I long to drink of Your living water that will never run dry. As I drink from the river of Your Spirit, may Your truth bubble forth from within me, transforming my life and touching those around me. Father God, in Yeshua's name I ask You to help me stay thirsty, so I can receive more and more of You!*

Use Your Authority

> Behold, I have given you authority to tread on serpents and scorpions, and over all the power of the enemy, and nothing will injure you.
>
> —LUKE 10:19

GOD CREATED THE heavens and the earth for you and me. He created the plants, the fish, the animals, and the birds, and He made them all for you and me. After He created the plants and the animals, after He separated the night from the day and the waters from the land, He put mankind on the planet. And He said to the man and woman, "Name everything. I've given you authority to have dominion and reign over My creation."

This is not only literal but is also a type and shadow of the nature of the authority and victory that we have been called to in the spiritual realm. Because of sin, man's relationship with God was broken and his authority was lost. But through Yeshua HaMashiach, that relationship has been restored. And in that restoration, we're brought back into the place of authority that God established for us at the beginning.

God has given us victory over all the power of the enemy through our relationship with Him in Messiah Jesus. We need to continue to develop a triumphant mindset. Paul the Hebrew *shaliach* (apostle or messenger) said in Ephesians 2:6 that we have been "raised up with Him, and seated...with Him in the heavenly places in Christ Jesus." So be bold and take authority in the spirit over the darkness of fear, worry, and hate. Break accusation off your life. God has given you mastery over the enemy. We are born of God's very life and light. The Spirit we have received is uncreated and everlasting. The light within us shines in the darkness, and the darkness cannot extinguish or overcome it. Let's take authority.

> *Father God, I declare the truth of Your Word today—that You have given me power to tread on serpents and scorpions and over all the power of the enemy, and nothing shall by any means harm me. I believe that You have given me authority in Messiah Yeshua, whose death and resurrection triumphed over the enemy. Because I am born of You, that victory is mine too. I will be bold and brave and use the authority I have been given by You, in Jesus' name.*

Newness of Life

> Therefore if anyone is in Christ, he is a new creature; the old things passed away; behold, new things have come.
>
> —2 CORINTHIANS 5:17

ARE YOU CONSTANTLY being changed? As new creations in the Lord, we are continually being renewed and transformed day by day. Old things are passing away. We're not the same people today that we were ten or even five years ago. Why? Because we're being changed from the inside out.

Now, you might say, "Well, yeah, everyone changes in five years." But I'm not talking about changes in one's physical appearance, personal life, or career. The kind of change I'm talking about results from the very *zōē* life of God—the literal Spirit of the eternal God—living continually inside us. Because He's always new, you and I are being changed into new creations.

Again, this process of being changed into a new creation is something that is not static. It's not that we suddenly change from one thing to another and then stay that way forever. Rather, because God is alive and is always causing newness of life to bubble up in us, we as new creations are unceasingly being changed, like a flower that constantly blooms new petals. God is making us more and more like Him each day. He's taking us from glory to glory (2 Cor. 3:18) so we fulfill the destiny He mapped out for us when He wrote our names in the Lamb's Book of Life (Rev. 21:27).

My friend, you are much more than you know. You are supernatural. There is a seed inside you that is perpetually sprouting newness of life. Say yes to God. Surrender to His will and His ways so the seed of eternal life that He has placed in you can be given expression in and through you.

> *Father God, I don't want my life to be static. I long to be continually changing to become more like You, to reflect Your character and be conformed to Your image. Lord, I want to become the person You purposed me to be and fulfill the destiny You mapped out for me. Father, Your Word says You have ordained days for me and that they are written in Your book (Ps. 139:16). Help me to maintain a posture of surrender so You can change me from the inside out. Dad, I want to fully become who You have ordained me to be.*

DAY 34

Be United in Love

For the whole Law is fulfilled in one word, in
the statement, "You shall love your neighbor as
yourself."

—GALATIANS 5:14

I DON'T KNOW ABOUT you, but I am very convicted by
this verse because I am basically selfish. I have to overcome my own nature, and I am overcoming, but it is a
slow and challenging process. It takes resolve and self-
sacrifice. It involves picking up our cross, denying ourselves, and following Him (Matt. 16:24).

I've been walking with the Lord now since 1978. And
the older I get in the Lord, the more I understand that
love is the greatest thing of all. When I was younger in
the Lord, so many issues kept me divided from people.
Now I realize that maturity is to walk in unity. And what
produces unity? Love.

Today's scripture teaches us that in the same way we
take care of ourselves we need to take care of others. We
need to give consideration to those around us. If you want

people to be considerate to you, then you need to also be considerate to them.

This verse presents another paradigm: we are to love our neighbor as ourselves. But wait, what if we don't love ourselves? If we hate ourselves, that self-hatred is going to reflect onto the people closest to us. We need to work on letting God love us so we can be healed of self-rejection and then be equipped to love others.

I want to encourage us today to walk in love, because love is what brings everything together. Some people are looking for reasons to be divided. They're looking for ways to produce discord. Mark my words, that's of the devil. Yeshua prayed to the Father in John 17:23 that His sons and daughters would walk in unity and love. As you and I put our minds to this purpose, we are going to ascend in His power. Let's go up the mountain of love.

> *Father God, help me to love others as You have loved me. Heal every wound that has caused me to hate myself, even in subtle ways, so I can love my neighbor as myself. Help me to see myself as You do and to see others as You see them so that I can experience a greater measure of Your Spirit and glory.*

Let Him Teach You

Teach me Your way, O LORD, and lead me in a level
path because of my foes.

—PSALM 27:11

IF YOU'RE ANYTHING like me, you want God to teach
and train you. You want to follow the straight-and-
narrow path that leads to His heart. But do you realize
that discipline is one of the tools HaShem uses to teach
and train us?

Proverbs 3:12 tells us that "whom the LORD loves He
reproves, even as a father corrects the son in whom he
delights." The writer of Hebrews said the same thing,
"For those whom the Lord loves He disciplines, and
He scourges every son whom He receives" (Heb. 12:6).
Because of His love for us, the Lord uses discipline to
teach us His way, nurture us, and protect us.

Of course, our Father uses many means to teach us.
He teaches us through His Spirit. He teaches us through
His Word. He teaches us through circumstances, people,
and suffering. Hebrews 5:8 says of Jesus, "Although He
was a Son, He learned obedience from the things which

He suffered." Every method God uses to teach us is for the same purpose—so that we will be transformed. Even Yeshua continued to grow in strength and wisdom (Luke 2:40).

The more we're taught and the more we yield to His instruction, the deeper we'll enter into the essence of Yeshua. This is why Father's discipline should be understood and received as a blessing. He disciplines every true child of His so He can release His fullness and goodness into our lives. God's discipline brings us into His blessing.

Father God, I cry out to You today. Teach me, O God, and lead me in Your way. Father God, discipline and nurture me. Teach me by Your Spirit and Your Word, and bring into my life whatever I need to follow the level path that leads straight into Your heart, Abba. Straight into Your bosom.

DAY 36

God Is With Us

Behold, I am with you and will keep you wherever you go, and will bring you back to this land; for I will not leave you until I have done what I have promised you.

—Genesis 28:15

THIS VERSE CONTAINS one of the most beautiful promises in Scripture. In these words spoken to Jacob is a promise for you and me. Yeshua said to you and me, "I will never leave you nor forsake you" (Heb. 13:5, NKJV), and God has promised us that He will complete the good work He began in us (Phil. 1:6). So you see, we really can apply this scripture the Father spoke to Jacob over our own lives as well.

You see, the Bible tells us that God is the author and the finisher of our faith (Heb. 12:2). Our Father is the Potter, we are the clay, and He is going to have His way in our lives (Isa. 64:8). The more we cooperate with Him, yield to Him, and put Him first, the easier the journey becomes and the faster the Father accomplishes His will in our lives.

Furthermore, Jesus said, "Lo, I am with you always, even to the end of the age" (Matt. 28:20). Even as Father was with Jacob wherever he went, so too it is for us today. Make no mistake: wherever you go, God is there.

God is already here, and He is already there! Keep confessing and affirming this—not only when life is easy but through the hard times as well. As you do, the roots of your faith will grow deep, and you will drink more and more of the well of His eternal life.

> *Father God, thank You for being with me and keeping me wherever I go. Help me to surrender to You and cooperate with You so You can accomplish Your will in my life. Awaken in my heart an expectation that You will fulfill every promise You have made to me. I confess that the One who called me is faithful, and I know that You will complete the work You started in me. Thank You, Abba, for loving me. I love You, my daddy God.*

Divine Satisfaction

> Go forth from your country, and from your relatives and from your father's house, to the land which I will show you.
>
> —GENESIS 12:1

IF YOU ARE bored right now in your Christian walk, if you feel that your relationship with God is stagnant, I want you to know that you do not have to stay stuck. If you will completely surrender yourself to God, the Father is going to bring you into a new realm of experiencing His glory, abundance, and eternal life. But you have to let go of where you are and yield to and follow Him.

If you are so concerned about what people think about you that you won't step out of the crowd to be different, you are going to stay stationary and unsatisfied. However, if you are willing to let go and obey Him, even if it does not make sense at the time, God is going to bring you into something fresh, new, and superior to where you are now!

You and I should be seeking to have an experience like Abraham's. He was willing to leave what he was comfortable with, forsake all that made him secure in the natural, and not consider what others thought—because he trusted God. To receive something more of God, to obtain the extraordinary, we cannot be concerned with our comforts or being different.

If we are too afraid of standing out or of taking a step of faith like Abraham did, God is unable to do what He wants to do for us because we are holding on to where we are. If we hold on to where we are, how can we come out of that place into a new thing? We have to trust HaShem, let go, and then follow Him where He leads us. This can involve either our internal thoughts and attitudes or our external circumstances.

God's Spirit is living, active, and real. We can truly have divine satisfaction and be led into an abundant life but only if we pursue Him with our all. Even though it can be scary, be assured that there is a reward on the other side!

> *Father God, I want more of You, more of Your color in my life. I choose to follow You as Abraham did. I let go of the things that make me feel secure in the natural, and yield to You instead. I love You; I want You. I will let go of and stop clinging to where I am and follow You to where You will lead me.*

Expect Christ's Return

Therefore be on the alert, for you do not know which day your Lord is coming.

—MATTHEW 24:42

THE LAST THING Yeshua HaMashiach told us in the Scriptures is, "Behold, I am coming quickly, and My reward is with Me, to render to every man according to what he has done" (Rev. 22:12).

Jesus is going to return when mankind is not looking for Him. He said His coming will be like when a thief enters someone's house at night. No one expects a thief to be coming. If they expected the thief, they'd stay up all night standing guard. That's what Jesus' coming will be like. He is going to come at a time when the world is not looking for Him. He could come any day—even right now. Jesus said, "Behold, I come quickly," meaning get ready. We need to live in such a way that we are ready for Him whenever He comes, even if it's today.

Beloved, are you ready? Have you dealt with every known sin in your life? Are there things in your life that God has been speaking to you about, things you know you need to repent of but have not? To repent means to turn from darkness, disobedience, and evil to follow Jesus and walk in His ways. I'm speaking to myself as much as to you when I ask, Are there things in our lives that we know need to be changed and yet haven't changed?

Ask yourself what would happen if Jesus came right now. Are you confident that you would go to heaven? The Bible says, "Strive to enter through the narrow door; for many, I tell you, will seek to enter and will not be able" (Luke 13:24). Messiah said to be on the alert. Be ready. Not everybody who confesses that they believe in Yeshua's return will be saved by Him. Jesus illustrated this when He gave us the parable of the ten virgins. All ten were waiting for their bridegroom, but only five had prepared themselves and were able to enter his presence when he finally came. (See Matthew 25:1–13.)

Jesus is coming back, and we must be ready. Let's prepare in advance for the coming of our King.

> *Father God, I don't want to be like the five virgins who got tired of waiting for the bridegroom. I want to be awake and expecting the return of my Messiah. Father, the apostles lived with a supernatural expectation that Jesus would return in their lifetime. Help me to also live with a supernatural expectancy that Jesus will return in my lifetime. Come quickly, Lord Yeshua.*

Purpose in the Pain

The LORD restored the fortunes of Job when he
prayed for his friends, and the LORD increased all
that Job had twofold.... The LORD blessed the latter
days of Job more than his beginning.

—JOB 42:10, 12

YOU PROBABLY KNOW many people who have biblical
names—Jacob, Daniel, Joshua, Luke, John, Esther,
Ruth, Deborah, Mary. There are even people named Israel.
But one biblical name I've never heard a parent give their
child is Job.

Many of us know the story of Job. The book begins by
saying Job was the most righteous and wealthy man of all
the people of the East. He was a pillar in the Lord, and it
was clear that God had blessed him. But one day when
the angels of the Lord appeared before HaShem, Satan
appeared along with them. And the Lord said to Satan,
"Have you considered My servant Job? There is no one like
him on the earth, a blameless and upright man" (Job 1:8).

"Yes," Satan replied, "but You protect him. No wonder
he loves You! Stretch forth Your hand against him, and

we'll see if he still loves You." (See Job 1:9–11.) As the story goes on, we find that the Lord gave Satan permission to attack Job, and the attack was severe. Job lost his family, his health, his reputation—he lost it all. This is hard for us to understand, which is why I think not many people name their children after Job.

But Job's life had a very happy ending. At the end of all his pain, Job told the Father, "Before this, I had heard about You, and I believed in You. But after going through this and coming out the other end, now I know You for myself." (See Job 42:5–6.) At the close of the book, we find that not only were Job's fortunes restored to him, but they were restored even beyond what he had originally.

If you're going through a trial today, regardless of how severe it is, if you will hang on to the Lord through it, you're going to come out the other end as gold refined in the fire. Beloved, your pain has a purpose. Nothing will be wasted. Nothing will be lost. It will work for good in the end.

Father God, You waste nothing. You use every trial, every hardship, every difficulty I face in my life. I am going from glory to glory as I cling to You. Thank You, Father, for giving purpose to my pain.

A Compassionate Father

The LORD, the LORD God, compassionate and gracious, slow to anger, and abounding in lovingkindness and truth…who forgives iniquity, transgression and sin; yet He will by no means leave the guilty unpunished.

—EXODUS 34:6–7

WHEN GOD SPOKE His name to Moses in the Book of Exodus and disclosed His nature, the very first characteristics of His nature are revealed: compassion and grace.

HaShem is a good God who delights in loving His chosen ones. He is merciful and slow to anger. He is not a God who erratically loses His temper, but rather He is filled with goodness, long-suffering, and love. And notice in our verse today that the Lord is "*abounding* in lovingkindness and truth." What does *abounding* mean? It points to something that is bubbling up, overflowing, and more than enough. Our God is an astonishing Father, running over with more than enough compassion and grace to meet all our needs!

But let's also notice the next thing our God makes known about Himself: "Yet He will by no means leave the guilty unpunished." Think about this. God is, first of all, compassionate, but secondly, He is just. We need to understand His essence, ways, and actions from these two perspectives. The Father is first of all merciful. That is why He sent our Messiah, Jesus. If He wanted to just show justice, He never would have sacrificed His Son for us. He would have just destroyed mankind for their sin and not provided a path for redemption. But because God is *compassionate* and *gracious,* He provided a way for us to turn to Him through Yeshua.

God loves you and me. But when He stands at the door of men's hearts and knocks (Rev. 3:20) and is not received in, He has no choice but to execute justice, condemning those who will not receive His grace (Rev. 20:15).

> *Father God, I confess that You are compassionate and gracious, slow to anger, and abounding in lovingkindness and truth. Let me always respond to Your grace and never take it for granted. You are a good Father, and I don't know what I would do if not for Your mercy and gentleness. Thank You, Lord, for providing a path to redemption so I can enjoy these times of fellowship with You. I love You.*

Be Conformed to God's Word

And do not be conformed to this world, but be transformed by the renewing of your mind, so that you may prove what the will of God is, that which is good and acceptable and perfect.

—ROMANS 12:2

THE TRUTH IN this verse is simple and profound. If we don't transform our minds by rejecting the mind of our culture, we're not going to have the spiritual discernment that is required to perceive God's will and leading in our lives.

This is certainly true of many people today. As a spiritual leader, I've observed many single younger people who love God. But because sexual immorality is so common in the culture today, many of these younger people compromise in this area and then justify it in their own minds, saying, "It's OK because we love each other." And sometimes as a result they fall away from Jesus. This is just one of many examples of how we can reject God's Word and then excuse ourselves because our culture says, "It's OK."

If our minds are programmed by the world rather

than the Word, we're not going to be able to discern the appropriate will of God. Whether it's sexual sin or some other issue, when we're conformed to the spirit of this age rather than God's inspired, written Word, we can't discern God's heart and will convince ourselves that what is wrong is really OK.

Hebrews 4:12 says the "word of God is living and active and sharper than any two-edged sword, and piercing as far as the division of soul and spirit, of both joints and marrow, and able to judge the thoughts and intentions of the heart." When we allow God's Word to get into our hearts and psyches, it changes us.

Beloved, we don't determine truth or where we are in our walk with God by comparing ourselves to other people or to this world's cutlure. We measure ourselves by comparing ourselves to God's Word. So I want to encourage you today not to get sucked into the present culture. Rather, resist the spirit of the age and be conformed to God's Word. Spend time in scriptural literature every day.

> *Father God, may Your Word set the standard for my life and not the world around me. Help me today to resist the temptation to follow the pattern of this world and instead let Your Word renew my mindset. I want to be in alignment and in agreement with You, in Yeshua's name.*

Exchange Anxiety for Peace

Be anxious for nothing, but in everything by prayer and supplication with thanksgiving let your requests be made known to God. And the peace of God, which surpasses all comprehension, will guard your hearts and your minds in Christ Jesus.

—PHILIPPIANS 4:6–7

WE NEED TO believe that we can experience the peace of God. But hear this—we have to do something. Paul said in 1 Timothy 6:12, "Fight the good fight of faith." Like King David who "encouraged himself in the LORD" (1 Sam. 30:6, KJV), we have to activate ourselves. We need to take the initiative to be spiritually aggressive and shift the spiritual atmosphere around us from anxiety to confidence and peace.

This is a battle. You don't move from 100 percent anxiety to 100 percent peace all of a sudden. You don't go from being a zero to a hero in a day, a week, or even a year. God didn't drive out Israel's enemies all at once but "little by little" (Exod. 23:30). We progressively move into less anxiety and more peace. Yes, it is a fight, but we will overcome as we pour our lives out to the Lord and communicate with Him every day, talking with Him even more than we talk to our friends, parents, or spouse. As we share our life with the Lord, are honest with Him, and invite Him to help us, we will see recovery and more and more be freed from anxiety.

How does this happen? The Spirit of the Lord enters our lives, and through our dependence on Him, doors are created within us so that God gets more and more possession of our mind, disposition, and emotions. As that happens, we will find ourselves girded with more and more of the peace of God. This is a real transaction. We give Him our anxiety, and He gives us His peace.

So today I want to encourage you to fight the good fight of faith. If you'll war for this, you're going to find as time goes by that you are walking in a heavier and heavier anointing of the very shalom of Jesus Himself.

Father God, I cast my cares on You. I choose to be bold and confident in You. I declare Your Word over my life. I will be strong and courageous by the power of Your resurrection, King Jesus. I will fear no evil, for You are with me. Thank You for delivering me from anxiety and giving me Your peace.

Choose to Love Him

For in Him we live and move and exist, as even some of your own poets have said, "For we also are His children."

—ACTS 17:28

You and I are the pinnacle of all God has made, and it's clear He saved the best for last. Why do I say this? Because He created us in His image, and today's verse tells us that we exist *in Him*.

All that God has made is in Him because He upholds everything He has created by His power. (See Hebrews 1:3 and Colossians 1:17.) But while God's creation is in Him, it is also separate from Him. We're separate from Him in the sense that we're unique and have our own will. In other words, you can choose to do this or to do that. God doesn't force you to wear a green coat or a white coat. You have the freedom as an individual to choose how to dress, which car to buy, or what to eat for breakfast.

That is by design, of course. Father God loves us, but He never wanted to force us to love Him in return.

He wants us to choose to love Him. A real love relationship involves two unique persons with separate wills. For a love bond and relationship to take place, each unique individual in the relationship must "will it." When we choose to love our Father, it literally moves His heart.

Because of God's great love for us, He sent Yeshua and has given us the freedom and opportunity to choose to love Him back. In fact, this is all He really wants from you and me. This is why Yeshua taught that the greatest commandment is to love Adonai with all our heart, soul, and mind (Matt. 22:37).

> *Father God, thank You for loving me. In You I live and move and have my being. I choose to love You in return. Father God, may my choices show that I love You. Help me to honor You with my life.*

He's Here!

I am the LORD, and there is no other; besides Me there is no God. I will gird you, though you have not known Me.

—ISAIAH 45:5

GOD'S NAME, WHICH is translated as "LORD" in today's verse, is from what we call the tetragrammaton. It consists of the four Hebrew letters *yud*, *hey*, *vav*, and *hey*—YHWH, or Yahweh—and it carries with it the idea of "to be." It conveys the concept of God as "who is and who was and who is to come" (Rev. 1:8). And there is no other God beside Him.

What the Lord is saying to you and me is that although we cannot see Him and are often not aware of Him, He is here and strengthening us. Beloved, God is alive. He is present and amongst us, wanting to breathe newness of life into you and me. Even as a river is constantly flowing and the water is always new, so is God always new and always moving, and He wants to work in your life today.

I want to challenge you today to believe this. Believe God for a miracle. Believe Him to do something new for you. The apostle Paul wrote that God "is able to do exceedingly abundantly above all that we ask or think, according to the power that works in us" (Eph. 3:20, NKJV). Believe Him for more. Let Him raise Your expectations of what He can do in your life.

Ask Him to open your heart, and believe Him to change you. Yeshua came to live inside you. He came to set you free. Believe He is working in your life, guiding you and strengthening you—and as a result, you will be delivered and liberated. He wants to bring you into a greater victory over the powers of darkness that have been oppressing you.

> *Father God, help me to believe there is more—more strength, more power, more revelation, deeper intimacy, and a closer walk with You. Raise my expectation that You are going to do exceedingly abundantly above all I could ask or think according to the power that is at work in me. I ask, Father, that You bring me to a place of victory in every area of my life.*

Be a Warrior

The LORD is a warrior; the LORD is His name.
—EXODUS 15:3

SOME PEOPLE ARE born with more of a warrior spirit than others. We're all wired differently. Some people are more outgoing, and some are more gentle. You've probably heard people say, "I'm a lover, not a fighter." Regardless of our natural bent, we have to be able to take out of the reservoir of the Lord within us that which is necessary for every situation. And sometimes it's necessary in life to be a warrior—to make decisions and act in a way that might be very hard in the natural.

Think, for example, of Abraham. Abraham was a kind and loving person, but there were certain times in his life when he had to be a warrior in order for him to obey God. For instance, the Lord spoke to Abraham and said, "I want you to leave your father, your relatives, and this place that is familiar to you, and I want you to follow Me." It took a warrior spirit for Abraham to rise up, cut off his past, and enter into the new reality and destiny that God had for him.

Now consider this: There may be certain things in your life that you've been tolerating, and God doesn't want you to tolerate them any longer. There may be certain changes in your life that need to be made, but you haven't made them because you're afraid they're going to hurt somebody. If you have been passive in your spirit, I want to remind you today that one of the attributes of your Father is that He's a warrior, and as His child, that same warrior strength has been imparted to you.

So I say to you today in the name of Jesus: Rise up and be the warrior that Father has called you to be. Make those decisions Yeshua is asking you to make. Take those actions in your life that HaShem is asking you to take. You have the Spirit of God living in you. That means you have a warrior spirit. "The LORD is a warrior, the LORD is His name" (Exod. 15:3).

> *Father God, Your Word declares that the righteous shall be as bold as a lion (Prov. 28:1). Help me to walk in Your strength and to be a warrior. In my weakness, Lord, Your strength is made perfect. So I ask You today to help me rise up in Your strength and do the things You are calling me to do, even if they are hard and may hurt.*

Walk by Faith

For we walk by faith, not by sight.
—2 Corinthians 5:7

WHAT EXACTLY IS faith? Hebrews 11:6 says, "Without faith it is impossible to please Him, for he who comes to God must believe that He is and that He is a rewarder of those who seek Him." That means faith, first of all, is to believe there is a God, even though we can't see Him. God's Word also teaches us that we should have faith in the fact that He rewards those who seek Him.

Some people find it hard to believe God exists, but isn't it harder not to believe? When we look at creation, the evidence of God's existence is all around us. In fact, Romans 1:20 tells us that God's "invisible attributes, His eternal power and divine nature, have been clearly seen, being understood through what has been made, so that they are without excuse."

Sometimes a wound or hurt caused by the enemy creates a block in someone's soul, but everyone deep down in their heart of hearts knows there is a God. When we hear the awe-inspiring crash of the ocean against the shore, when we look at the endless sky, we can't help but see the obvious. Creation is God's handiwork, and it reveals God's power and nature.

Once we are confronted with the reality that God exists, we must choose whether to follow Him. That is the second element of faith. First we believe God exists, then we must act on that faith by doing what pleases Him and believing He will reward us.

I want to encourage you today to not only believe there is a God but also trust that He's good and He loves you. He sees you; He's watching you and has numbered every hair on your head. He's closer to you than your own breath, and you exist in Him. Beloved, believe that He is and that He's going to reward you for seeking Him.

Yes, Father God, I believe You're real. I see proof of it in creation. I exercise my faith right now and believe that You love me. Thank You for being closer to me than my own breath. Help me to live my life in a way that pleases You and to diligently seek You.

This Is a Fight

For sin shall not be master over you, for you are not
under law but under grace.

—ROMANS 6:14

THERE'S A TOPIC we don't often hear about in the
church today—sin. To many in our culture, the word
sin is like a prehistoric term. They put *sin* and *dinosaurs*
in the same category. But the Bible tells us that sin has
separated humanity from God. Sin looks like this: God is
moving in one direction, and we are going in another. It
creates a break in the relationship. That's what happened
with Adam and Eve in the Garden of Eden, and that's
what we're battling with today.

In Genesis 4:7 we read, "Sin is crouching at the door;
and its desire is for you, but you must master it." Sin is
a power, and it is being projected onto you and me. The
enemy is trying to lead us away from God by enticing us
to make wrong choices, develop wrong attitudes, think
wrong thoughts, and live in rebellion. And the outcome is
always the same. Sin brings isolation, accusation, shame,
and finally death, because it leads to separation from God.

Yes, church, we're in a fight! This is why Paul said *sin is not to be our master.* Some people think they're supposed to yield to whatever they feel because they think their identity is defined by their feelings. But this is not true. God's Word defines how we should live. We've been called to repent of sin, return to the Creator, and live according to God's Word. But we don't have to do it alone. We do it through God's grace. If we have a *yes* in our hearts, if we strive to overcome sin, God is going to meet us and help us, and we will overcome!

Beloved, it won't happen overnight, but if you're committed to overcoming sin, if you're committed to putting God's Word into practice in your life, you will enjoy the fruit of everlasting life forever and ever! You see, the wages of sin is death, but the free gift of God and the reward of walking by the Spirit is everlasting life and peace.

> *Father God, help me to not live according to my feelings but to walk according to Your Word. I want to be pleasing in Your sight and not let sin be master over me. Strengthen me. I ask You, Father, to help me put Your Word into practice in my life so I can enjoy the fruit of choosing You, which is love, joy, peace, and everlasting life.*

Free to Love and Be Loved

> For I am convinced that neither death, nor life, nor angels, nor principalities, nor things present, nor things to come, nor powers, nor height, nor depth, nor any other created thing, will be able to separate us from the love of God, which is in Christ Jesus our Lord.
>
> —ROMANS 8:38–39

WE SOMETIMES HAVE a hard time loving ourselves, which can make it difficult for us to receive love from others. It can even cause us to struggle with receiving God's love. Father wants us to be able to receive His affection for us. He longs to cleanse us of self-rejection, delivering us from this defiled spirit of darkness so we can receive all of His love.

Abba wants to remove the stains of self-rejection and past hurts by the blood of Jesus and the sanctifying work of the Holy Spirit. Father's purpose is to bring us into His marvelous light so we can experience His acceptance. The primary way our Father causes us to grow in His love is by bringing us into the revelation that He cherishes us.

The Lord wants us to know that He desires us, treasures us, and loves us unconditionally. When we know this, we will be free to both receive and give love.

We have to rise up and break off the spirit of self-rejection! You must resolve to agree with Yeshua that you are beautiful—beautiful in Him and beautiful to Him. The Father wants you to know that you are lovelier than the most magnificent flower or the most delicate butterfly. You are more amazing than a hundred roaring lions, more majestic than a soaring eagle, because you are the crown of God's creation (Gen. 1:27) and the apple of His eye (Ps. 17:8).

God created you in His own image, and the very Spirit of God resides in you! You are wholly desirable to God. He sees Himself in you, and you are lovely to Him. From the top of your head to the bottom of your feet, you are special to Him (Song of Sol. 7:1 10). God loves you, and He wants you to overcome self-contempt by embracing how beautiful and desirable you are to Him. His love for you is a flame of fire. The Father wants to consume us with His love, setting us free to love ourselves and others.

Father God, I reject Satan's lies, and I believe that You love me. I believe a supernatural cleansing and transformation is taking place in my life right now. I receive Your love, my God. I love You! In Messiah Yeshua's name.

Don't Fear the Darkness

For behold, darkness will cover the earth and deep darkness the peoples; but the LORD will rise upon you and His glory will appear upon you.
—ISAIAH 60:2

THE DARKNESS IS growing thicker in and on the earth. In fact, it has been overtaking the world so quickly that if we realized what was happening, it would take our breath away. Satan is gaining dominion in the atmosphere of our planet. The Bible says that in the last days, He that restrains, speaking of the Holy Spirit, will no longer restrain (2 Thess. 2:6–7). What this means is that in the last days (which is today), the Holy Spirit will withdraw His influence, and as He does, evil will rise in that vacuum and become predominant.

Today's verse says that darkness will cover the surface of the earth, even deep, thick darkness. This is what is happening now, and it's only going to get worse. It's going to become more intense than you can imagine, and it's going to happen more quickly than you'd expect. But hear this: the Lord said He will shine upon you! So let's not be afraid of what we see happening around us. The Bible says, "You are not to say, 'It is a conspiracy!' In regard to all that this people call a conspiracy, and you are not to fear what they fear or be in dread of it" (Isa. 8:12). You and I are to fear the Lord alone. And when we do, He will become our sanctuary.

Beloved, as the world continues to spin out of control, as chaos increases, as corruption becomes more severe, as all the things spoken of in Scripture concerning the end times come upon us, do not be afraid. Even though the darkness is getting deep and thick outside in the world, you have another destiny. God's glory will continue to be your portion and will shine upon you even in the midst of the darkness. In all these things we overwhelmingly conquer, so be of good cheer and do not be afraid. He that "is born of God overcomes the world; and this is the victory that has overcome the world—our faith" (1 John 5:4).

> *Father God, I know Your light shines brightest in the darkness. Help me to be a light in this dark world. My destiny is not to live in fear but to reflect Your glory. I know I am more than a conqueror because greater is He who is in me than He who is in the world. Thank You, Abba Father, for shining the light of Your love upon me and being my portion and protection. I put my hope in You.*

In Spirit and Truth

But an hour is coming, and now is, when the true worshipers will worship the Father in spirit and truth; for such people the Father seeks to be His worshipers.

—JOHN 4:23

JESUS SAID, "WHEN I am raised to life again, you will know that I am in my Father, and you are in Me, and I am in you." (See John 14:20.) Yeshua's use of the word *know* indicates that this relationship is something that is to be intimately experienced and felt.

Our faith rests not just in spirit and not just in truth, but in the combination of the two. The point I want to make is that we should not limit our relationship with God by focusing only on having correct doctrine. We also need to spiritually experience God. Simply put, Father has blessed us to be able to sense Him.

What would you think of marriage if the relationship with your spouse had no feeling? Relationships involve feelings, and feelings make us alive! I am not saying we are to be led only by our feelings. But those who never feel, sense, or experience anything intuitively in their relationship with God are missing something.

I want to know Yeshua in me and around me. I want to sense His glory and experience His love, peace, joy, and power. All these things require an experience. They cannot just be in the mind; they have to be sensed in our hearts and spirits. Yeshua sent His Spirit to continue to reveal Himself to us (John 16:13–14). In other words, Jesus said: "I am going to send you the Spirit, and the Spirit will make Me real to you. The Spirit will take of Me—My very nature, My very thoughts, My very heart, My very feelings—and He will impart them to you."

As believers, our primary goal is to come into a greater realization of God's Spirit and presence in our lives—to know not only the truths of His Word but to also know His presence in reality. Beloved, we can truly experience God and His Son—in spirit *and* in truth. Believe it!

> *Father God, I am excited to experience Your presence. I want to feel Your Spirit and sense Your activity in my life. I want to know You in both spirit and in truth, both with my head and my heart. I pray today for a fresh anointing and touch from You, in Yeshua's name.*

DAY 51

Satisfied in Him

Now on the last day, the great day of the feast, Jesus stood and cried out, saying, "If anyone is thirsty, let him come to Me and drink. He who believes in Me, as the Scripture said, 'From his innermost being will flow rivers of living water.'"

—JOHN 7:37–38

YOU'VE PROBABLY HEARD the saying that what we all have in common is death and taxes. That may be true, but at a deeper level, what all humanity shares in common is a desire to be fulfilled, complete, and happy. In John 4:14, Yeshua said, "Whoever drinks of the water that I will give him shall never thirst; but the water that I will give him will become in him a well of water springing up to eternal life." Rivers of living water will eventually cause our souls to become so satisfied in HaShem that we will lose our interest in anything else. We will not be attracted by anything the world has to offer because we will find the deepest possible satisfaction in the One who created us for Himself.

So if you're thirsty, Jesus is inviting you to come and

drink. How do we do that? We talk to Him. We share with Him the truest parts and deepest longings of our souls. We tell Him the things that are hurting us, the things that make us sad, the things that make us angry, and the things that confuse us. We get honest with Him, opening our souls to Him so there are no secrets.

Yeshua defined eternal life in John 17:3 as knowing God. In other words, the satisfaction from the living waters is realized through relationship. To know God as our Father, a real person, and to know how much He loves us and who we are to Him fulfills the deepest longings and needs of our souls.

Beloved, the Father wants to be one with you. Yeshua said, "I and the Father are one," and He prayed that you and I would experience this same oneness (John 17). By being open and honest with God, baring our souls to Him every day and being thankful for all He has done for us, we will receive what Jesus spoke of and be filled with living waters.

> *Father God, open my eyes to see the ways I can be even more transparent with You so I can come into a deeper place of knowing You. I want to find my identity in You and experience Your love.*

You Are a Victor in Yeshua

> No temptation has overtaken you but such as is
> common to man; and God is faithful, who will
> not allow you to be tempted beyond what you are
> able, but with the temptation will provide the way
> of escape also, so that you will be able to endure it.
>
> —1 CORINTHIANS 10:13

WHAT I LOVE about this verse is that it recognizes that regardless of how we're being tempted, God is still actively involved in our lives. When we're being tempted, He's already there with us—in the middle of losing our temper, in the middle of having a bad attitude. In the middle of whatever it is, God is right here with us.

And I want you to know that when you are tempted, God's feelings of love for you do not change. He will give you the way of escape if you will keep clinging to Him even in the middle of the temptation.

Now, you may feel like you're failing. You might think, "I'm clinging to God and I'm praying, but my attitude still stinks. There are still words coming out of my mouth that I know are not in alignment with love and truth." But I believe that if you will keep hanging on to God, if you will keep praying for the situation, He will strengthen you through the process, and you will overcome.

At the end of the day, God is going to perfect you and complete the work He started in you. Whatever temptation you're dealing with, you will overcome it because God will make a way out. It may not always happen immediately. There may be a process involved. But the Father will complete the work He began in us. He will cause us to overcome. You and I are victors in Yeshua.

And when we have sinned, we may think that God is angry with us and wants nothing more to do with us. But the Bible says that "if anyone sins, we have an Advocate with the Father, Jesus Christ the righteous" (1 John 2:1).

> *Father God, thank You for not giving up on me and for making a way of escape when I am tempted. Help me to know and believe that Your love for me never changes. Father, help me to keep clinging to You. I believe that as I continue to press on, You will strengthen me, and I will overcome all sin.*

A Matter of Perception

For our struggle is not against flesh and blood, but against the rulers, against the powers, against the world forces of this darkness, against the spiritual forces of wickedness in the heavenly places.

—EPHESIANS 6:12

I'VE KNOWN FOR decades that the Word of God says my fight is not against flesh and blood—it's not against people or circumstances but against a living force of darkness. But how often have I failed to live that out? How often have I thought and behaved as though my enemy is a specific circumstance or a particular person?

Beloved, we need to war to gain spiritual sight, revelation, and understanding so we will comprehend that our true battle is not against flesh and blood. You see, the real battle is not in what's going on; it's in the way that we perceive what's going on. That's the whole key. This is what happened when Jesus was being tried before Pilate. (See John 19:1–16.) Pilate couldn't understand why Yeshua wasn't afraid of him. Pilate told Jesus, "Don't You know that I have the power to crucify You? Why aren't You afraid? Why aren't You trembling before me?" Jesus said, "You would have no power over Me unless it was given to you from above." Jesus understood that His fight was not against flesh and blood.

God is calling us into the next level of revelation. Our warfare is not in the low level of flesh and the material world. Our warfare is in our comprehension of what is going on—this is where we need deeper revelation. Whatever your battle is right now, are you perceiving it through the lens of the power of darkness or through the eyes of the Holy Spirit? Remember, two people experience the same event in totally different ways What is the dif ference? Their perception.

> *Father God, I'm thankful that You have raised me up in Yeshua. Give me a spirit of wisdom and revelation to comprehend the real battle and to see things through the eyes of the Spirit. I declare that my war is not against flesh and blood, people, and circumstances. I am in a spiritual battle. Open my eyes today, Father, so I can walk in the light of truth and in the victory of King Jesus.*

Something Worth Living For

> While we look not at the things which are seen,
> but at the things which are not seen; for the things
> which are seen are temporal, but the things which
> are not seen are eternal.
>
> —2 Corinthians 4:18

Let me ask you a question: When you think about the things in life that really matter, that really add value—beyond having your basic needs for survival met—are they things that are seen or things that are unseen? I'd say they are unseen. For example, can you see love? In a sense, you can see the effects of love, but love is spiritual. We need to build our lives upon those things that are not seen, eternal things such as love, joy, and peace. Everything in the visible world is only temporary and fades away, but spiritual qualities are the soul's true food.

I once heard a man talk about buying a new refrigerator when he was a young adult. This was one of the first major appliances this guy ever bought in his life, and he was so excited about it, he kept going into the kitchen and looking at it. He even got up in the middle of the night to go down to his kitchen to look at it again and marvel at its automatic ice maker and chilled water features. But eventually his love for his refrigerator went cold. (I hope you got that joke.) The point is that our excitement over everything in the material world wears off. You get a new car and you just love it so much at first and maybe you still appreciate it over the years, but eventually the newness fades away.

Let's make sure we're investing our time and our talent, our love, affection, and treasure in spiritual things that will last forever. We're not going to be able to take our houses and cars with us into eternity. "Therefore if you have been raised up with Christ, keep seeking the things above, where Christ is, seated at the right hand of God. Set your mind on the things above, not on the things that are on earth" (Col. 3:1–2). Let's make our lives count by living for things that are worth living for.

> *Father God, help me to set my affection on things that are eternal and not invest too much of my time, talent, and treasure in things that will fade away. I want to pursue Jesus and to know Him in "the power of His resurrection and the fellowship of His sufferings" (Phil. 3:10). I want my life to count for eternity.*

Cling to God

> After you have suffered for a little while, the God of all grace, who called you to His eternal glory in Christ, will Himself perfect, confirm, strengthen and establish you.
>
> —1 PETER 5:10

THE MESSAGE IN this verse is one that some may find hard to hear. Why? It says that in order to be perfected, confirmed, and established, we need to suffer a little while. Suffering involves the testing of our faith. It is easier to get revelation in our heads than to know it deep down on the inside. There's a difference between getting a revelation in our minds and having it established in our hearts.

I can personally attest to the fact that sometimes my revelation is greater than my experience. A lot of the revelation I receive from the Lord needs time and personal experience in order for it to go deeper than my mind and actually be established in my soul. This is why God allows us to suffer sometimes. He puts us in difficult situations so the revelation we've received will be put to the test.

What do I mean by "put to the test"? Does that mean God wants to see whether we're going to pass or fail? No. It means God is going to put us in a situation that requires us to use the revelation He has given us. Once we've used the revelation in a challenging circumstance, it gets rooted inside us.

Beloved, God is using everything that's going on in your life for your good, to perfect you and conform you to the image of Christ. We all will go through trials because trials establish us and conform us to Jesus' image. So be encouraged today. Life wasn't meant to be easy. Just keep clinging to God, and as you do, you will become and look more and more like Jesus.

> *Father God, I know You use the challenges I face in life for my good, to help me grow and root Your truth deep in my heart. Help me to cling to You and never let go. Abba, I want Your Word to go from my head to my heart. I say yes to You and give You permission to do with my life whatever You want. Establish Your Word in the center of my being.*

Rejoice and Give Thanks

Rejoice always…in everything give thanks; for this
is God's will for you in Christ Jesus.
—1 THESSALONIANS 5:16, 18

THIS PASSAGE IS short, but it presents us with a major
challenge.

Rejoice always. Do you rejoice always? I don't. I am
definitely working on it, though. Not long ago, the Holy
Spirit communicated to me audibly in my sleep and said:
"Rejoice continually, and you will overcome every situation." I know it isn't easy to do; in fact, it's far from easy.
But rejoicing in the midst of difficulty releases God's
power and enables us to overcome.

This leads us to the second part of the passage, which
tells us to give thanks in everything. This means that we
thank God not only before we have a steak dinner but in
all situations. We must believe that when we're walking
through a difficult season, God is working something in
us that can be obtained only by clinging to Him in the
darkness. We must trust that even though the circumstance feels unpleasant, God is doing something good

in us through it. When we know that, we can give Him thanks even in hard times.

If you're in a difficult season, just stop for a second and say, "Father God, thank You for this season because I believe You're doing something in me that I could not receive if things were easy." The Bible says God causes all things—not just the good and pleasant experiences, but all things—to work together for good to those that love Him and are called according to His purpose to conform us to the image of Christ (Rom. 8:28–29).

God wants us to have enough faith in Him to thank Him always, regardless of what we're going through in life. Why? Because we believe He's good and He's doing something good for us. As we do this, beloved, we're going to go from depth to depth and from strength to strength. And when we get strong, we'll be happy.

> *Father God, Your Word says Your will for me is to rejoice continually and always have a thankful spirit through Messiah Jesus. Father God, I confess that I have not always lived up to this. I thank You for understanding the battle I'm in against the enemy. But I realize this is no excuse. Father, strengthen me to live according to Your Spirit and Your Word.*

See Yourself in the Light of God's Word

For God has not given us a spirit of timidity, but of
power and love and discipline.

—2 TIMOTHY 1:7

THE WORD OF God is like a mirror. We look into it,
and it shows us who we are. We study it, and it helps
us discern where we are in life so we can make any necessary changes. God wants us to see ourselves in the light
of the mirror of His Word. Considering this, beloved,
today's verse reveals to us that if we're living in timidity,
fear, shame, or inferiority, we have to war against it and
overcome. Why? Because those things do not come from
God.

Some people say, "This is just the way I am. I've always
been shy and withdrawn." But that's not good enough.
God loves us too much to leave us where we are. God gave
us His Word to call us up to a higher level—where He
wants us to be. God has not given us a spirit of timidity, so
if I'm naturally a timid person, I need to break the spirit

of timidity off me because I am a new creation in Christ Jesus. "Old things are passed away; behold, all things have become new" (2 Cor. 5:17, NKJV).

We don't define ourselves by who we are in the natural. We may have been born one way, but that's just the beginning of the story. We've been born again, which means we're being changed. We're going from grace to grace. We're looking unto Jesus, the author and perfecter of our faith (Heb. 12:2). In Christ, we don't have a spirit of fear; we have a spirit of power, love, and self-discipline. Don't make excuses and tell yourself this is just the way you are. God is calling you to something bigger and better. You don't have to change yourself; God's Spirit is at work in you, empowering and renewing you day by day, and as you look to Him, you will be changed.

Let's get in agreement with God's Word and believe we are who HaShem says we are. Let's confess it and declare it. Let's practice walking in it. As we do, we'll be transformed into His likeness and reach our destiny, which is to shine like the stars forever and ever.

> *Father God, I don't want to live beneath Your best for me. Use the mirror of Your Word to show me who I am, where I am, and any course corrections I need to make. Help me to not only know the truth in my head but also believe it in my heart.*

A Fundamental Truth

For by grace you have been saved through faith;
and that not of yourselves, it is the gift of God; not
as a result of works, so that no one may boast.
—EPHESIANS 2:8–9

SOMETIMES PEOPLE ARE skeptical of the word *theology.*
They think focusing on theology will cause their faith
to become dry and stale. But theology isn't a bad word;
rather, it's the system through which we understand
truth. In fact, correct theology is necessary because our
theology—the way we think about God—defines how we
relate to Him.

Today's verse encapsulates a foundational theological
concept: we are saved by grace through faith, and the
faith that saved us didn't come from us; it's the gift of God.
The Lord relates to us by grace. It's His unmerited favor
upon us that has brought us into a relationship with Him.
Some world religions believe God relates to people based
on their works. But Yeshua dying on the cross to save
us right where we are shows us that God doesn't love us
based on our works. He loves us based on His grace; He

created us, and He loves us where we are. The Scripture says, "God demonstrates His own love toward us, in that while we were yet sinners, Christ died for us" (Rom. 5:8). He truly loves us and is fond of us.

To grasp this is fundamental, because if you don't understand this, you'll run from God when you sin. You'll live in shame and isolation. But when you understand the unmerited love of God that has been poured out upon your life, you'll be able to be open and transparent before God, which is necessary to build a relationship with Him.

Paul says the faith that saved us isn't something we manufactured; it is a gift from God. In other words, God desires us so much that He even gave us the ability to believe in Him. So, beloved, know today that God loves you. He loved you so much that He gave His only begotten Son, not only to save you from your sin but so that He could be with you forever. Messiah Jesus didn't die just to forgive you; He died to marry you. (See Revelation 19:9.)

> *Father God, thank You for making it possible for me to spend eternity with You. I know that it wasn't because of anything I've done but it's because of Your grace that I am saved. Help me to always remember that our relationship is not based on my works but on Your unmerited love and gentleness toward me.*

Total Dependence

Who is a rock, except our God, the God who girds
me with strength and makes my way blameless?
—PSALM 18:31–32

THERE IS NO rock, nothing solid or stable in life, except
God. Messiah Jesus gave us this parable to illustrate
this fact: "Therefore everyone who hears these words of
Mine and acts on them, may be compared to a wise man
who built his house on the rock. And the rain fell, and the
floods came, and the winds blew and slammed against
that house; and yet it did not fall, for it had been founded
on the rock. Everyone who hears these words of Mine and
does not act on them, will be like a foolish man who built
his house on the sand. The rain fell, and the floods came,
and the winds blew and slammed against that house; and
it fell—and great was its fall" (Matt. 7:24–27).

Yeshua was David's life. The air David breathed was
the *ruach* (breath) of the Spirit and the Word of God.
This is what made him a great king. David's relationship with Yeshua was so dependent and tender that
David compared it to that of a child depending on

his mother. David wrote in Psalm 131:2–3, "Like a weaned child rests against his mother, my soul is like a weaned child within me. O Israel, hope in the Lord from this time forth and forever." Even though David lived during Old Testament times, we know that he knew Yeshua as Messiah because of what David said in Psalm 110:1, "The Lord says to my Lord: 'Sit at My right hand until I make Your enemies a footstool for Your feet.'" Yeshua declared in Luke 20:41–43 that David was referring to Him in this psalm.

Through Yeshua, the Lord was continually nurturing David because of David's dependency upon Him. And because David was totally dependent, he was made strong in God's power, and his way was made blameless. You see, the key to entering into God's victory is humility, and humility is dependence upon the Lord. In loving and clinging to the Rock of Israel, you too will become very mighty.

> *Father God, I need You. You are the source of my strength. You are the air I breathe. You are my life and my rock. I want to place myself completely in Your hands, to be totally surrendered to You. Spirit of God, train me to know that I can do nothing without You. And make me know that through You I can and will conquer and overcome all.*

Love One Another

This is His commandment, that we believe in the name of His Son Jesus Christ, and love one another, just as He commanded us.

—1 John 3:23

It's an ugly truth, but the fact is, we as human beings are selfish by nature. You see, by nature we are in the flesh, and the nature of the flesh is selfish. It is wired to satisfy its own desires. Our physical appetites for food, sex, and the like are self-oriented. But God is calling us to a supernatural life where we transcend to truly love one another.

This is why Jesus said, "If you love those who love you, what credit is that to you? For even sinners love those who love them" (Luke 6:32). Even sinners love their friends because being with friends makes us feel good. We don't love our friends just for who they are; we love them because of how having them in our lives makes us feel. As hard as it may be to realize this, there is truth in it. But Jesus said, "I'm calling you to something bigger. I'm calling you to love your enemies." (See Luke 6:35.)

Yeshua also said, "Greater love has no one than this, that one lay down his life for his friends" (John 15:13). We must understand that love involves sacrifice, and sacrifice oftentimes is doing something that doesn't feel good.

Loving others may mean visiting somebody we don't really feel like going to visit. Or it may mean being patient with someone, because love is patient and kind (1 Cor. 13:4). We sometimes make Christianity about going to worship services and enjoying our favorite worship songs. I love that myself, but walking with Jesus is more than just feeling His presence when the worship music is playing. Walking with Jesus involves loving one another and showing love to our enemies. In both cases, love involves sacrifice.

Beloved, let's strive to grow in love. Let's examine our hearts and ask Yeshua to help us love others as He commanded us to.

Father God, I know it's Your will that I love others as You first loved me. Give me the grace and strengthen me to do the things that may be uncomfortable so I can demonstrate Your love to others. Help me to listen and be sensitive to others. Make me patient and kind, long-suffering and humble. Instead of seeking my own way, help me to yield to Your will.

DAY 61

Focus on His Beauty

The heavens are telling of the glory of God; and
their expanse is declaring the work of His hands.
Day to day pours forth speech, and night to night
reveals knowledge. There is no speech, nor are
there words; their voice is not heard.

—PSALM 19:1–3

WE CAN DISCOVER a lot about the nature of God
and who He is by simply looking at His glory
revealed in creation. Not long ago I visited Israel during
the springtime, and all around me new life was emerging.
The plants and flowers were absolutely gorgeous. With
their vibrant orange, yellow, and purple colors, they were
powerfully declaring the glory and beauty of God.

Israel is also a famous migration area; birds fly in and
out of the country as they go from country to country.
I saw so many beautiful, colorful birds—in blues, reds,
greens, all the colors of the rainbow in different patterns—
and they were shouting the glory of God.

God is beautiful. Don't you love that about God? David
said, "One thing have I desired, and that is to be in Your

presence and to gaze upon Your *beauty* all the days of my life." (See Psalm 27:4.) And I have found that if we choose to focus on His beauty, we will know and feel that He is with us.

Sometime back, the Lord specifically spoke to me in my sleep and said, "When you feel lonely, focus on My beauty, and you will know that I am with you and that I am real." So, beloved, if you feel lonely today, just look out upon creation. Focus on something beautiful that God has created, and I am confident that you will perceive that God is much closer than you may have realized. God is speaking through His glory in the earth. Let's listen.

> *Father, one thing do I desire of You, and that is to behold Your beauty and abide in Your presence. So many people feel alone in the world. As I see Your beauty in creation, help me to realize how close You are and how much You love me. Your Word declares that the heavens are telling of Your glory. Lord, help me to always be aware of Your beauty and glory, which You have revealed to me in the world around me.*

A Unique Anointing

Thus says the LORD of hosts, "In those days ten men from all the nations will grasp the garment of a Jew, saying, 'Let us go with you, for we have heard that God is with you.'"

—ZECHARIAH 8:23

ZECHARIAH HERE IS speaking of what the Scriptures call the "last days" or the "end of the age." The things the Bible prophesied thousands of years ago about the last days are coming to pass in our lifetime. Daniel, for example, prophesied that in the time immediately preceding the Lord's return, people would be traveling to and fro, and our knowledge would be greatly increased. That's what's happening right now. Airline travel can get us anywhere in the world in less than two days, and we are living in the midst of the information age, with rapidly advancing internet and digital technologies.

These are the last days, and one of the things Zechariah prophesies about these times is that believers will recognize God's supernatural call upon the Jewish people. You see, when Joseph was in Egypt, the whole nation was elevated because of him. Egypt was about to enter a season of famine, but because of the advice Joseph gave to Pharaoh, Egypt was able to survive the famine and prosper. Later, when Egypt threw the Jewish people out, their nation was destroyed. There's a special anointing on the Jewish people. This is why the Lord said those who bless the Jewish people will be blessed (Gen. 12:3).

Jesus said in John 4:22, "Salvation is from the Jews." Let's recognize the key role the Jewish people play in these last days. The anointing of the Lord flows into the earth through specific channels, and one of those channels is Jewish believers who are living in the world today.

I want to encourage you to pray for the Jewish people. Pray for breakthrough in Israel. Pray for revival among young people in Tel Aviv. Beloved, let's pray that the Jewish people would recognize Yeshua as the Messiah and come to salvation, because when they do, it will be like life from the dead for the entire church (Rom. 11:12–15).

Father God, thank You for the anointing You have placed on the Jewish people and the blessing they've been to the world. I pray for a supernatural breakthrough in Israel. May the Jewish people recognize Yeshua as their Messiah and usher in Your return.

DAY 63

Called to Repentance

Or do you think lightly of the riches of His kindness and tolerance and patience, not knowing that the kindness of God leads you to repentance?

—ROMANS 2:4

TODAY PEOPLE RARELY hear a message on repentance. They're hearing that God wants to bless them and extend His favor toward them, but they're never being called to repent. They're not being called out of sin or encouraged to rise to a higher standard.

In today's verse, Paul explains that the love, kindness, and patience we've experienced in our lives are designed to convince us of God's love for us, and our response should be to turn to Him, repent, and commit our lives to Him. God doesn't bless immorality. He doesn't bless selfishness. He doesn't bless everybody going their own way and doing what's right in their own eyes. We're called to repentance—to turn to Him and follow His way. John the Baptist and Messiah Jesus declared the same message: "Repent, for the kingdom of heaven is at hand" (Matt. 3:2;

Matt. 4:17). We can't take this lightly. God will judge sin. He is not mocked.

David was a man who committed atrocities in his life. But when he realized the depth of the evil things he had done, his response was to repent. That should be our response too. I want to encourage you, beloved, if there are things in your life that are crooked, make your way straight, for the coming of the Lord is soon. God has been patient with you this long, not because He's blessing your sin, but because He wants you to become convinced of His love for you. He does this so you'll turn your heart over to Him and repent.

Let's take this to heart. Let's examine ourselves and ask Abba God to show us what is within us and what crooked and broken places in our lives need to be made straight. Now is the time to take inventory because Messiah Jesus is coming back soon. (See Revelation 21 and 22:12, 20.) Soon it might be too late.

> *Father God, thank You for Your kindness and patience toward me. Search my heart and reveal anything in me that is not in alignment with You so I can repent. Father, I want to please You. And I want my life to be a sweet fragrance to You. Continue to transform me into Your likeness.*

Share the Source of Your Hope

I will lift up my eyes to the mountains; from where shall my help come? My help comes from the LORD, who made heaven and earth.

—PSALM 121:1–2

I HAVE FOUND THAT many Christians are afraid to share the hope of Jesus with others. They think they are going to offend someone or be rejected, but I have oftentimes seen the exact opposite to be true. When I'm in a restaurant, for example, and look for a way to lift up Jesus to the waiter or waitress, I have found that the majority of the time, the person is encouraged and inspired by what I share. Why? Because they're struggling in life, and they need hope and encouragement.

The psalmist in today's verse knew that God truly helped him. Messiah Jesus is the hope and help of the world, and we need to share His hope with others. More and more people are taking their own lives in this generation, and the ones committing suicide are getting younger and younger. How sad that we live in a culture in which we have young children, barely even teenagers, taking their own lives because they have no hope. Why is this happening? Because God has been taken out of the culture. He's been expelled from the school systems. He's been evicted from government properties. He's been excised from businesses. He's even missing from a lot of churches. The atmosphere is godless.

The psalmist truly experienced that his help comes from the Lord. He knew that as long as we have God, we have hope, because nothing is impossible with God. Don't ever give up on God, beloved. The only place where there is no hope is in hell. As long as you're not in hell you have hope. I want to encourage you to keep talking to Jesus. Yeshua said, "Knock and the door will be opened. Ask and you will receive." (See Matthew 7:7.) Beloved, don't give up. Your hope is in Jesus. "He who believes in Him will not be disappointed" (1 Pet. 2:6).

"I will lift up my eyes to the mountains; from where shall my help come? My help comes from the LORD, who made heaven and earth" (Ps. 121:1–2).

> *Father God, I ask that You give me courage to share with others the source of my hope. Show me strategies to share Your truth with those I come in contact with.*

Drink of Eternal Life

He will be like a tree firmly planted by streams of water, which yields its fruit in its season and its leaf does not wither; and in whatever he does, he prospers.

—PSALM 1:3

WHAT HAPPENS WHEN we make the Lord first in our lives, when we make seeking His truth and His presence our number one objective? The psalmist says we prosper and experience success. Yeshua said, "But seek first His kingdom and His righteousness, and all these things will be added to you" (Matt. 6:33).

I'm not talking about material success necessarily. I'm talking about God's Spirit of everlasting life living in us and through us. The psalmist says when we strive to put God first, when there's a big *yes* in our hearts unto Jesus and we yearn to do what's right (even though sometimes we fall), Yeshua will forgive us and renew us. And we will continually bear fruit in every season of our lives. We'll be changed from glory to glory, grace to grace, and strength to strength. Even though our outer man may be decaying as we age, our inner man will be renewed day by day. We'll keep getting younger and younger in the spirit. Our lives will have an effervescent youthfulness to them even when we're old. Why? Because we're drinking of eternal life.

So let me ask you a question today. What source are you drinking from? Are you drinking from the world? Are you drinking from negativity, ungodly relationships, cynicism, sarcasm, bitterness, and accusation? Are you filling yourself with Hollywood entertainment and secular music? Or are you drinking from the wellspring of God's Word, Spirit, and the fellowship of believers in His Son? The choice is before us. The Lord says, "I have set before you life and death, the blessing and the curse. So choose life in order that you may live" (Deut. 30:19).

Beloved, we can't have it both ways. I challenge us today to discipline ourselves and choose life so we can live abundantly in Yeshua.

> *Father God, help me to drink from the well of Your Spirit. Try my heart and make it known to me when I am drinking from wells that lead to death. More than anything I want You to have Your way in my life. I want to be renewed day by day as I yield my will to You and honor You with my life.*

See Beyond the Offense

> But Jesus was saying, "Father, forgive them; for they do not know what they are doing."
>
> —LUKE 23:34

THIS IS A familiar passage for many people—Yeshua was on the cross, dying for the sins of the world. And as He was making a way for us to spend eternity with the Father, people were on the ground mocking and laughing at Him. Then just as Jesus was about to take His last breath He prayed, "Father, forgive them, for they don't realize what they're doing."

That verse helps me to remember that when people do destructive, evil things that hurt me, oftentimes they don't even understand why they're doing what they're doing. The people committing evil against us are not rooted in the truth. They're not whole. Usually they are hurt people who are hurting others. They are broken people who, as a result of their brokenness, now victimize others.

Sometimes we need to get beneath the offensive behavior and try to gain insight into why people behave the way they do. We may wonder why someone said that offensive thing. A lot of times it's because they're afraid and insecure. But we don't perceive their insecurity, their fear, their inferiority. All we hear are the insults.

Beloved, let's pray that Father God will help us to see beneath the offense and understand who these people that hurt us really are. When we know who they really are and why they're doing what they're doing—that it's a result of their own hurt and brokenness—we'll be like Yeshua, who looked on at those that mocked, insulted, and crucified Him and said, "Father, forgive them; for they do not know what they are doing."

> *Father God, I ask You right now for a spirit of discernment, of wisdom and revelation to be able to see through the surface and penetrate the realms of darkness to see people for who they are so I can forgive and love them. Father, I ask You for compassion for humanity. In Yeshua's name.*

DAY 67

Under His Shelter

He who dwells in the shelter of the Most High will abide in the shadow of the Almighty.

—Psalm 91:1

I F A TERRIBLE hailstorm is coming and you're outside, what do you do? You find shelter. That is the concept being presented in this verse. To dwell under the shelter of the Most High means we actively come under His covering in our lives by choosing to cling to Him. It's not something that just automatically happens. Coming under the shelter of the Most High is a choice we need to make. We need to purposely look to the Lord to be our refuge, our covering, our shelter.

We see this posture in the life of Moses. When the Lord commanded Moses to lead the children of Israel out of Egypt, Moses said to the Lord, "Unless You go with me, I am not going to do it." (See Exodus 3–4.) Moses would only go out on that mission if he knew God was with him. That's how I feel in my life. I'm afraid to live life without God. I look around me at all the negative things that could happen—all the tragedies, all the accidents, all the uncertainties, all the sicknesses, all the dangers that are out there—and I know my only security is my relationship with God.

Beloved, we need to embrace Him as our shelter. When we do that, the Lord responds to that commitment, that humility, that dependency we have on Him by covering us with His wings. In that place of security, we experience the benefits of Psalm 91. The Lord becomes our refuge and safety. He delivers us from every trap and protects us from attacks. His faithfulness becomes our shield and much more. (Read Psalm 91.)

God loves you. Run to the safety of His covering. Let's cling to Him every second of every day. As we do, a wonderful opening will be developed in us, which will become a channel through which God's power and fullness will flow into our lives, and His strength will protect us.

Father God, I run to the safety of Your covering. Hide me under the shelter of Your wings. With all the dangers in the world, You are my safety. I choose to cling to You. I cling to Your love and protection. I cling to Your unmerited kindness and Your guidance. Like Moses, I don't want to take a step unless You're with me. Father God, You are my certainty. I put my trust in You.

Include God in Everything

In all your ways acknowledge Him, and He will make your paths straight.

—PROVERBS 3:6

IN LIFE THERE are so many decisions we need to make every single day. All day long we're faced with choices, and frankly, sometimes I don't know what the right choice is. I don't know the end from the beginning. So the only thing that gives me peace is if I acknowledge God throughout my day and ask Him to guide me and help me to make the right decisions.

We don't know how everything we face in life is going to play out. So how do we have confidence? How can we be secure? How can we walk in a way that keeps us from being anxious? It's by acknowledging God in all we do. Proverbs 3:6 says, "In all your ways acknowledge Him, and He will make your paths straight."

That's why oftentimes throughout the day, I'll just stop and pray. I'll gather with the people I work with, and we will pray together before we start filming or making decisions. Why? To acknowledge the Father in all we're doing so we can make the most of the opportunities He has given us to serve Him and to be a blessing for Him to those He wants to reach through us.

I want to encourage you today to include God in everything. This might sound comical to you, but I ask the Lord what clothes to wear every day. I ask the Lord what I should eat at night. I ask the Lord whether or not I should have dessert. I include Him in everything as much as possible, and the result is the same as it is for everyone who acknowledges Him—He makes our paths straight and prospers us.

Beloved, God loves you. He is just waiting for you and me to fully love Him back and include Him 100 percent in our lives. When we do, the fullness of HaShem's love and blessing will cover us.

> *Father God, I ask You to help me keep You at the center of all I do. Help me to include You in everything. You've numbered every hair on my head, so I know You care about every detail of my life. Help me to seek Your counsel, even in the small things. Thank You, Father, for making my paths straight as I depend on and keep my eyes on You. In Yeshua's name.*

Stick Up for the Underdog

Open your mouth for the mute, for the rights of all
the unfortunate.

—PROVERBS 31:8

GOD ANOINTED SOLOMON, who wrote the Book of Proverbs, with eternal wisdom that surpassed all the rest of humanity. One of the things Solomon advised God's people to do is to open our mouths for the mute and the less fortunate. To put it simply, we are to stick up for the underdog.

Our God is a father of the underdogs. He cares about the oppressed, the weak, the widows, and the orphans. Consider what He did for ancient Israel. They were the fewest people in all the earth. God saw them being persecuted and mistreated by the Egyptians, and He heard their cry and rescued them. After God rescued them, He said to Israel, "You know what it's like to be mistreated, and I don't want you ever to forget it. I want you to stick up for the rights of the poor and the unfortunate."

We lead such busy lives, and often we're so stressed with taking care of the details of our own lives that we don't think about how to help others. We can be so self-absorbed. Compounding this, the culture we live in is putting many of us under such extreme pressure that we are becoming even more hard-hearted. But we need to overcome the stress of the culture and be sensitive to others.

I want to encourage you to consider someone who is struggling or hurting and help them. Look for someone you can speak up for, someone you can defend. That may mean financially supporting a humanitarian ministry or befriending someone at work, at your church, or in your neighborhood who you know is struggling. Jesus came as a servant of all, and as children of God, we must do the same. Beloved, become a servant. Look for people you can help, especially those who are struggling with physical, emotional, or financial hardships. This is what it means to be the hands and feet of Jesus.

> *Father God, You care for the oppressed, disadvantaged, struggling, poor, and weak, and You want me to be mindful of the least of these too. Lord, Your Word says that You reward those who give even a cup of cold water to someone in need (Matt. 10:42). Father, help me to look beyond myself to see the needs of others. Let me not be so busy today that I overlook an opportunity to share Your love with someone in need. Father, make me a servant, in Yeshua's name.*

Be Anxious for Nothing

Be anxious for nothing, but in everything by
prayer and supplication with thanksgiving let your
requests be made known to God.

—PHILIPPIANS 4:6

Two things immediately stand out to me when I
read this verse.

First, I see the Lord telling us not to be distressed. I
don't know about you, but I have to fight to not be afraid.
When things happen in life that we feel are out of our control, the natural human tendency is to be uneasy about it.
But this verse is telling us to guard our hearts and be anxious for nothing, but rather stay rooted in God's peace,
His shalom.

There are probably things in your life right now that
you're uptight about. Maybe you are a student nervous
about an exam. Or perhaps you're anxious about a health
concern that you or a loved one has. Maybe you're fearful
about money. Whatever you're dealing with, take a step
back, pause for a second, and lift the concern up to Him.

That brings us to the second insight from this verse. It

tells us that when we're anxious, we should not only talk to God about it, but we should ask for His help with thanksgiving. When we thank God, we remind ourselves of all that He has done in the past, which raises our expectation of what He will do in the present and future. By faith we thank Him that He hears us and will be faithful to us.

Beloved, the Father doesn't want us to be anxious. He wants us to trust Him and live in the security of His love and care for us. His Word says He takes care of the birds of the air, and not one sparrow falls to the ground without Him knowing it (Matt. 6:26; 10:29–31). If that's how He treats the birds, you can be confident that He is involved in your life and there is nothing for you to fear.

> *Father, forgive me, and please deliver me from anxiety. Help me today. I lift my concerns up to You.* [Say whatever your concern is.] *Father, I ask You to strengthen me with Your peace right now. I also want to come to You right now with a spirit of thanksgiving, praising You for Your faithfulness and all the things You've already done in the past. Father, I'm asking You now to give me faith in You in this situation. Father, help me. I repent of anxiety, worry, and fear; deliver me from this spirit. Help me to guard my heart.*

Created for One Purpose

All things came into being through Him, and apart from Him nothing came into being that has come into being.

—John 1:3

IN THIS VERSE, John is declaring that Yeshua is the Creator. Now, that may seem confusing because we know that God the Father is greater than all. Romans 11:36, speaking of the Father, says, "From Him and through Him and to Him are all things." But the Father created everything through His Word, and Yeshua is the Word.

"In the beginning was the Word, and the Word was with God, and the Word was God.…And the Word became flesh, and dwelt among us" (John 1:1, 14). These verses are powerful because they not only tell us that everything that has been created has come into being through Yeshua, but also that when Yeshua was lifted up on the cross, the Creator Himself was in Him. The Creator clothed Himself in humanity because of His love for those He created. He took our sin in His own body on the tree, and He did it to restore the pathway back to

Himself, which was broken when Adam and Eve sinned in the Garden of Eden.

This is the most important message in the world—we can be reconciled to God. The only way for you and me to be whole is to come into a relationship with the One who created us. It makes no sense to think we're going to find meaning outside of Him, because the One who created us made us for Himself. So if we want to be whole, we need to return to Father God through His Son. That means not just believing in Him with our minds. Biblical faith involves not just agreement with truth, but doing what that truth commands us to do. (See John 14:23.)

Beloved, God created us for Himself. We will not find ultimate meaning outside of Him. Let's get that straight and choose to walk down the straight-and-narrow path that leads to life.

> *Father God, You created me through Your Word, who is King Yeshua. From You, through You, and back to You are all things. I surrender to Your will and say yes to You today. I believe that my soul is only whole when it is united to You. I want to live in the fullness of Your purpose for creating me.*

God Is Our Defense

Do not deliver me over to the desire of my adversaries, for false witnesses have risen against me, and such as breathe out violence.

—PSALM 27:12

DAVID PRAYED TO Father God, asking for protection from his adversaries. You and I live in a different generation, and the details of our circumstances are somewhat different than David's, but fundamentally we are in the same boat as David. All around us are powers of darkness that want to destroy us, and sometimes these powers of darkness try to work through people.

That's why we need to depend on God for protection. God guards His children through His angels and by His Spirit, and we need to be cognizant of the fact that we need Him to be our defense. There are forces surrounding our lives that want to swallow us up. The devil wants to destroy God's children. He is an accuser. He steals, kills, and destroys, and many times he uses people to do so.

The Bible tells us in the Book of Revelation that when

Yeshua was born into the world, the dragon went after Him. But then God raised Him up to the right hand of the throne, and the Scriptures say that when the devil saw that Jesus was raised, he went after Jesus' offspring. That's Israel, and that's you and me. (See Revelation 12.)

So we can have confidence, beloved, that we're protected from the desire of the adversary. But we should also be cognizant of the fact that God's covering is the only thing keeping us protected. Let us, therefore, walk before Him with a spirit of love, honor, dependency, and holy reverence.

Father God, thank You for being my covering and delivering me from the desires of my enemy. I don't take Your protection for granted. You are my strength, and You uphold me with Your right hand. You are mighty, Lord. Your Word says, "Greater is He who is in you than he who is in the world" (1 John 4:4). So I stand confident and courageous as I go through this day because I know You go with me.

He Cares About Every Detail

> There is no fear in love; but perfect love casts out fear, because fear involves punishment, and the one who fears is not perfected in love.
>
> —1 JOHN 4:18

I HAVE OFTEN PRAYED for a deeper understanding of this verse. One thing it means for sure—when we understand how perfectly the Father loves us, we will not be afraid.

You see, Jesus said, "Are not two sparrows sold for a cent? And yet not one of them will fall to the ground apart from your Father. But the very hairs of your head are all numbered. So do not fear; you are more valuable than many sparrows" (Matt. 10:29–31). Getting hold of how intimately the Lord loves us and is involved in our lives dispels fear.

God cares about even the minute details of our lives. I know it's easy to say that; it's harder to really grab hold of that reality, especially when we're going through hard times. For example, sometimes I get attacked in my sleep with bad dreams that make me feel I'm a million miles away from God. I wake up in the morning and think, "Lord, if I'm so close to You, why did I have that dream? Where were You?" I have to fight to say, "Lord, even though it seemed like You weren't with me in that dream, I'm going to still believe that somehow You're completely, intimately involved in every detail of my life. Your love was hovering over me as I slept last night. I know the picture is bigger than what I'm seeing right now. Help me to understand how much You love me."

Beloved, we need revelation of how intimately involved in our lives God is and how deep is His affection for us. When we truly get this, we will fear nothing, because we will know we are not victims of circumstance but that God is in control, directing everything and completely watching over our lives.

> Father God, I ask that the fullness of the love You demonstrated when You sent Your Son to die on the cross for us would penetrate my heart and mind, so I will understand what You meant when You said perfect love casts out all fear. Father, I want to truly realize that there's not one part of my life that You're not with me in. In Jesus' name, Daddy, I ask You for great revelation of Your love.

The Paradise of God

And He said to him, "Truly I say to you, today you shall be with Me in Paradise."

—LUKE 23:43

IN LUKE 23, Yeshua was being crucified, and there was a criminal being executed on each side of Him. One of the criminals was mocking Him, and the other said, "Jesus, remember me when You come in Your kingdom!" (v. 42). And when the man put his faith in Yeshua in his dying moment, Yeshua told him he would from that day forward be with Him in paradise.

The Scriptures teach us that eye has not seen and ear has not heard the things that God has prepared for those who love Him (1 Cor. 12:9). The greatest things we have ever experienced in this world don't compare to what God's people are going to experience in the afterlife, the paradise of God.

Your greatest imagination of the world to come doesn't compare to how great eternity with HaShem is actually going to be. Again, the Lord says it hasn't even entered into the heart of man the things God has prepared for those who love Him. It's going to be so much better than the most amazing things we could dream.

I know life can be tough and each day can feel like a battle. The forces of darkness are powerfully moving all over the face of the earth, and every day you and I are in a fight. We have to overcome darkness and depression, anxiety and fear, chaos and lust, poverty and health issues, and so many other things that affect us while we live in this world. In the Book of Revelation, Yeshua said to the church at Pergamum, "I know where you dwell, where Satan's throne is" (Rev. 2:13). It's a tough journey that we're in down here, but Jesus also said, "Be faithful until the end, and you will inherit the Paradise of God." (See Revelation 2:7.)

Beloved, God has something great in store for you. Keep pressing on. It won't be long before you'll be with the Father and King Jesus in the Paradise of God.

> *Father God, help me to believe that nothing on this earth can compare to the beauty I will see in heaven. In Yeshua's name, help me to always keep eternity in my heart* (Eccles. 3:11) *and focus on being faithful to You while I walk this earth. I'm thankful, my Father and God, that when I complete the assignment You have for me here, the best is yet to come. In Yeshua's name.*

HaShem's Love Is Your Portion

My flesh and my heart may fail, but God is the strength of my heart and my portion forever.

—PSALM 73:26

IN TODAY'S VERSE, the psalmist is telling us that in those times in life when we run out of steam, when we have no power to continue, we should not fear because *God* is our strength and the portion of our lives. Isn't this an awesome thing to know? When we feel we have no more energy, the Lord will raise us up.

How do I know that? Second Timothy 2:13 says, "If we are faithless, He remains faithful, for He cannot deny Himself." When Israel felt they were alone in the wilderness and could not help themselves, the glory of God appeared in a cloud (Exod. 16:10), and you have a cloud of glory that is with you wherever you go. It is the Ruach HaKodesh, the mighty Spirit of God.

Because of your relationship with HaShem, you have a divine engine within you, so even when your heart and flesh fail, there's a life force within you that will keep you going, restore you, refresh you, and cause you to rise up out of the ashes.

Romans 8:11 tells us that "if the Spirit of Him who raised Jesus from the dead dwells in you, He who raised Christ Jesus from the dead will also give life to your mortal bodies through His Spirit who dwells in you." Elect one of God, you cannot be defeated. You're going to be raised out of every circumstance that threatens to overwhelm you. You're going to be brought out of it victoriously every single time because the same power that raised Yeshua from the dead lives in you!

Even when your flesh fails you, you have One living inside you who is your strength, and He is only going to lift you back up. "Though he may stumble, he will not fall, for the LORD upholds him with his hand" (Ps. 37:24, NIV). Let's grab hold of this truth today—the love of God is our portion, and love cannot fail us.

> *Father God, I'm thankful that although my flesh gets weak, You are my strength. Your love is my portion. I receive the truth that even if I stumble, I will not completely fall because You uphold me with Your hand. Father, I declare that I will not be defeated, because the same Spirit who raised Yeshua from the dead—the Ruach HaKodesh— lives in me.*

Be Careful With Your Words

Let your speech always be with grace, as though seasoned with salt, so that you will know how you should respond to each person.

—COLOSSIANS 4:6

THE BIBLE SAYS that our tongues are like the rudder of a huge ship. The ship may be massive, but it is only a small rudder in the very back that determines what direction the ship will go. Our tongues are the same way. Our bodies are big, but our little tongues literally determine the course of our lives.

One of the most significant things you can do to move into greater spiritual power in your life and abide in Jesus in a deeper way is to control your mouth. How do we do that? The Bible says, "Let no unwholesome word proceed from your mouth, but only such a word as is good for edification according to the need of the moment, so that it will give grace to those who hear" (Eph. 4:29). That means we must avoid saying negative things about people and circumstances whenever possible.

We can't always avoid having negative thoughts about a

person, and sometimes we want to complain about a situation we are facing. I have found that nine times out of ten, it's unprofitable to make that negative comment. The better thing to do is just keep our mouths shut if we don't have anything good to say.

Back in the 1980s, I pastored a church that held a talent show on the last day of every month. Anybody in the congregation could get up and sing a song or play an instrument, and it was always such a beautiful time of fellowship. One night I was driving home from one of the talent shows, basking in the presence of the Lord, and then I spoke a negative word about one of the participants. As soon as I did, the peace and sense of God's presence that I had been feeling completely left me.

That's what speaking negatively will do. So guard your tongue, because from it flow the issues of life (Prov. 4:23). Beloved, let's use our words to build people up. Doing this one thing truly will empower you in a remarkable way. Anybody can be negative; it takes God's *zōē* (uncreated, supernatural life) to be positive and bring the kingdom of God into the spiritual darkness.

> *Father God, help me to guard my words. I want to use my mouth to lift others up and not tear people down. I want to bring Your kingdom to bear wherever I am.*

Trust the Father's Love

I have been young and now I am old, yet I have not seen the righteous forsaken or his descendants begging bread.

—PSALM 37:25

SOMETIMES WHEN WE look around and see so much suffering and tragedy in the world, we don't understand. But we can't allow ourselves to believe what we see with our eyes and conclude that we can't trust God. We must believe God's Word. God's Word tells us He will never desert us.

Often when people look at the suffering in the world, they say, "How could God let these things happen?" I don't know the answer to that question, but I choose to focus on the Word of God. I want to seize His Word and not let what I see with my eyes confuse me. His Word tells me He loves His children and will take care of them. David said, "O God, You have taught me from my youth, and I still declare Your wondrous deeds. And even when I am old and gray, O God, do not forsake me, until I declare

Your strength to this generation, Your power to all who are to come" (Ps. 71:17–18).

We oftentimes have fears about the future. We fret and worry about circumstances we might face one day. But God is with us, and we can have confidence that He is going to be with us, taking care of us even until the end. Psalm 73:23 says, "Nevertheless I am continually with You; You have taken hold of my right hand." Think about how much worry we would break off our lives if we had the same confidence as the psalmist.

Beloved, let's stake our hearts in the soil that God's Word is true. He will never abandon His people. I want to encourage us today: let's not doubt Father's love!

> *Father God, You promised that You will never leave me nor forsake me. I put my confidence in Your Word, not in what I see happening around me. I will walk by faith, my Lord, not by sight. I trust Your wisdom, not my own. I will not lean on my own understanding. Father, You are my strength and my confidence. I will not fear bad news because my heart trusts You (Ps. 112:7). I will not fear, Lord, because I know You are with me.*

Build Bridges to Peace

Now I exhort you, brethren, by the name of our Lord Jesus Christ, that you all agree and that there be no divisions among you, but that you be made complete in the same mind and in the same judgment.

—1 Corinthians 1:10

O NE OF THE most important things in the heart of Father God is that His children walk together in unity. If you have children, you know how deeply you want your sons and daughters to get along. It grieves us as parents when our children fight. The same is true of our God.

During His high priestly prayer right before He was going to the cross and then to heaven, Yeshua prayed, "Father, make Your children one even as You and I are one." (See John 17:21.) Unity in the body of Messiah is one of the most serious things to our Savior, and oftentimes we don't carry His burden for oneness.

The apostle Paul prayed in today's verse that there would be no division among us. Now, of course, there are disagreements. We don't all need to have the same favorite color or the same taste in music. We don't have to agree on everything, but we must be of the same mind, wanting to be in unity and, whenever possible, not allowing the small stuff to separate us.

It's critical to have a heart that desires to get along with people and to, as much as possible, strive to be at peace with everyone. Jesus said, "Blessed are the peacemakers" (Matt. 5:9). So, beloved, I encourage you to resist division. Look for ways to be in agreement with others. Do what you can to create bridges of peace. Unity brings life; division brings death. As you look for ways to build unity in the body of Messiah Jesus, you're going to be rewarded for it, because unity is a very weighty matter to God and the Spirit.

> *Father God, I know that Yeshua said, "Blessed are the peacemakers, for they shall be called sons of God" (Matt. 5:9). I want to honor You by pursuing peace and walking in love. Just as You are one, help me to walk in unity with others. Give me the wisdom to find peaceful solutions in tense situations. Father, please help me not to get distracted by small disagreements. May I share Your burden for oneness in the body of Messiah Yeshua.*

Look Up

As He was sitting on the Mount of Olives, the disciples came to Him privately, saying, "Tell us, when will these things happen, and what will be the sign of Your coming, and of the end of the age?"
—MATTHEW 24:3

IN TODAY'S VERSE, the disciples were asking Jesus two questions: When are You going to return and what will be the signs of the end of the age? The answer to these questions is multidimensional. In Matthew 24, Jesus spoke of wars and rumors of wars; He spoke of famines; He spoke of people's hearts growing cold. He also spoke of lawlessness increasing and of many people falling away from the faith. All these things are coming to pass.

So much of what Yeshua prophesied two thousand years ago is going on in the world right now! Again, we're seeing in a very real way an escalation of events that point to Yeshua's return—disasters, earthquakes, conflicts over nuclear weapons, chaos in politics, deadly disease spreading across the globe. Even the pollution of our air and waters points to the fact that things are growing darker year by year—Yeshua is setting the stage to return!

As to the disciples' other question, "When, Yeshua, will You return," Jesus said, "Behold, I am coming quickly" (Rev. 22:7). So I want to encourage you to look up. Get ready. Messiah Jesus is coming back, and He's coming back for you and me. He wants us to remind ourselves of this. He wants us to live with a heavenly mindset, recognizing that this world is not our home. He wants us to live with a conscious awareness that even a cup of cold water given in His name will come with a reward.

He wants us to expect His return. God's purpose is that every generation will anticipate Yeshua's return in their lifetime. "The Spirit and the bride say, 'Come'" (Rev. 22:17). Beloved, get ready. Jesus is coming soon, and He's coming back for you and me.

> *I agree with the Holy Spirit and I say, "Come quickly, Lord Jesus. Come back to earth. Break in and deliver Your people from every bondage and from the power of darkness. Messiah Yeshua, establish God's kingdom on the earth as it is in heaven in my lifetime."*

Let Him Be Lord of All

"Bring the whole tithe into the storehouse, so that there may be food in My house, and test Me now in this," says the LORD of hosts, "if I will not open for you the windows of heaven and pour out for you a blessing until it overflows."

—MALACHI 3:10

I KNOW THIS VERSE has at times been used to manipulate people, and I know some may instantly feel offended when I use it. But the reality is that tithing is a very important subject, because if we're not surrendered to God in the area of our finances, we're not fully surrendered to Him.

The reason I believe tithing is so important is because it brings about surrender to God. You see, oftentimes we have a tendency to trust in our finances for security, so when we surrender our finances to God by tithing our income, what we're actually saying is, "Lord, I'm going to trust in You. You're the source of my security, not my finances." Tithing is not about legalism but is rather an act of love, honor, surrender, and trust. That's why Jesus said we can't serve both God and money (Matt. 6:24).

You see, tithing goes all the way back to the Book of Genesis before the Law was given when Abraham gave a tenth of all he had to the priest Melchizedek. And Yeshua affirmed it when He said we should show mercy, grace, and peace without neglecting the tithe (Matt. 23:23).

Not only that, but the Lord said when we yield our hearts to Him in this way, it comes back to us in "good measure—pressed down, shaken together, and running over" into our lap (Luke 6:38). This is because when we surrender to God in the area of our finances, we open our hearts for Him to pour back into it. Beloved, tithing takes faith, and when we operate in faith and open our hearts to God through tithing, we create a channel for Him to fill our lives with His.

> *Father God, I know You're calling me to make You Lord of every area of my life. Father, wipe away all the crutches I have relied on to feel secure, including myself and my finances. I surrender my finances to You, and I trust You to meet my every need. You take care of the birds; You will surely take care of me. Help me to never doubt You.*

Everyone Matters

And the eye cannot say to the hand, "I have no
need of you"; or again the head to the feet, "I have
no need of you."

—1 Corinthians 12:21

Years ago God gave me a dream in which I mistreated someone who had a physical challenge. When I wasn't sensitive to this person, the Holy Spirit withdrew His presence from my life. That dream has stuck with me for all these years because the Lord used it to show me how important it is that we be sensitive to everyone, especially those the world has cast down.

You see, in the natural world, the high and mighty give their attention to others who have status, money, fame, or authority. But often they don't pay attention to people they consider to be lower than they are—those who haven't advanced as far in their careers, reached a certain financial status, or achieved a particular level of education. This is often how the world works, but in the kingdom of God, we need to be sensitive to everybody. That is not only because God loves us all the same; it's also because each one of us has incredible value, and we need each other.

We're dependent on one another. People might look at me and think being in full-time ministry or on television makes me a big deal. But the truth is, there's no way that I could do what I'm doing without all the people who are playing their huge part to make it possible. It begins with my wife, Cynthia. If she was not a nurturing wife to me, ministering to me with just her presence in my life, there's no way I would be where I am in my life today. Yet for many years Cynthia was behind the scenes.

I am often the one standing on the platform. But it's possible that when Cynthia and I stand before our Creator, she might have a greater reward than I do. Beloved, we need to recognize that everybody is doing their part. There are people in your life you might need to be more sensitive to, people you might need to show more appreciation to. Let's not overlook anybody or take anyone for granted, because everybody is of supreme importance in the kingdom of God.

> *Father God, help me to see others the way You see them and value them the way You do. I want to recognize the part each person plays in Your kingdom. Make me mindful of the need to always be sensitive to others and appreciate them for who they are.*

Stand Still

> But Moses said to the people, "Do not fear! Stand by and see the salvation of the Lord which He will accomplish for you today; for the Egyptians whom you have seen today, you will never see them again forever."
>
> —Exodus 14:13

In the original, historical context of this verse, the people of Israel had come out of Egypt, and they were at the edge of the Red Sea, but they were trapped. They couldn't swim across the sea, and Egypt was chasing them from behind. They began to panic. At that moment, Moses boldly declared, "Do not fear but stand still and see the salvation of the Lord."

Sometimes God wants us to just trust Him and wait patiently for Him in confidence. There are going to be times when you don't have to do anything except to keep believing, keep trusting, keep resting, keep being expectant, and you're going to supernaturally see God move in your life and circumstances. There are many, many times in our lives when we have to act, but there are other times when the Lord is telling us, "Just stand still and watch what I do."

I have seen God do some things in my life when I was in a season of waiting on Him that I could never have accomplished in my whole lifetime by my own initiative. And like Israel, which stood still and watched their God deliver them from Egypt, you too will see God work in your life as you trust Him. God is delivering His people from every satanic oppression and demonic assault. The time is coming when you will be free indeed.

When we get to heaven, there will be no more tears, suffering, pain, sorrow, or sickness. Everything that's old will have passed away. Just as God told Israel they would never see their enemy again, He is bringing you and me into paradise, a place of joy and eternal freedom. Beloved, let's keep our eyes fixed on Messiah Jesus and watch Him bring us into paradise.

> *Father God, I confess that whom the Son sets free will be free indeed. I claim the freedom I have through Yeshua my Messiah, freedom from every satanic oppression and demonic assault. I declare my victory in Jesus' name. Father God, help me to stand in faith as I watch Your glory being released in my life.*

You Are His Bride

> "Then I passed by you and saw you, and behold, you
> were at the time for love; so I spread My skirt over
> you and covered your nakedness. I also swore to
> you and entered into a covenant with you so that
> you became Mine," declares the Lord GOD.
>
> —EZEKIEL 16:8

IN THE ORIGINAL context of today's verse, God is
speaking to Israel of His love for her. But through
Yeshua, Gentiles have been grafted into the common-
wealth of Israel, so this revelational word of God's love
applies to everyone who trusts in Him (Eph. 2:11–13). You
and I are the bride of God through Messiah Jesus.

The apostle Paul said, "For this reason a man shall leave
his father and mother and shall be joined to his wife, and
the two shall become one flesh. This mystery is great; but
I am speaking with reference to Christ and the church"
(Eph. 5:31–32). Paul used the image of a man and woman
becoming one in marriage to show us the type of union
we now have with the Lord.

The Bible says in Revelation 19:9, "Blessed are those

who are invited to the marriage supper of the Lamb." It's a mind-blowing reality to recognize that God loves us with a marriage type of love. He's not just the Lord in the sky who provides for all our needs. He's not just El-Shaddai, the Almighty; He's also the God who looks at us as His cherished spouse. We are His bride, and His banner over us is love. He not only meets our needs, but He also takes pleasure in spending time with us. Jesus didn't die only to forgive you of your sins; that was just the beginning. Ultimately He died to marry you.

Beloved, love is the core of our relationship with God. Let's have confidence in His love.

> *God, give me a revelation of Your Word so that I will truly understand that I am Your bride. Help me to comprehend that Your banner over me is love and You have brought me into a relationship with You in which You not only meet my needs but also take pleasure in me. Father, help me to receive this truth, not just in my head but in my heart. Let me know the width and height and depth of Your love for me. Father, fill me to overflowing. In the name of Yeshua, my Messiah, I ask and pray. Amen.*

Be a Witness for Him

But you will receive power when the Holy Spirit
has come upon you; and you shall be My witnesses.

—ACTS 1:8

AT PENTECOST (ACTS 2:1–31), God's people received His Spirit as an indwelling possession, and it marked the fulfillment of the Old Testament Shavuot. (See Leviticus 23:15–21.) Through the Holy Spirit, we now have intimate relationship with the Father.

There is no greater event in the history of the church, aside from the death and resurrection of Jesus, than the giving of the Spirit of God. When the Father gave us His Spirit, He gave us Himself. In His Spirit is love, power, joy, and victory! Through His Spirit we can go through, and get through, whatever tribulation we may be experiencing right now and whatever trials we will face in the future. But we cannot know the power of the Spirit unless we obey the Spirit. "For the one who sows to his own flesh will from the flesh reap corruption, but the one who sows to the Spirit will from the Spirit reap eternal life" (Gal. 6:8).

In today's verse Jesus commands us to be His witnesses. Beloved, we are not going to know the fullness of God's Spirit unless we are obedient to Him in the realm of witnessing. We have a mission in this world, and it is to be light in the darkness. You don't have to always give a complete presentation of the gospel. Just let your love for Jesus shine in both your words and deeds. Jesus said, "Let your light shine before men" (Matt. 5:16).

I want to encourage you to begin making Jesus known to the people around you in a stronger and more loving way. Now is the time to share Jesus with others and tell them of the power He has to change their lives. You can be a bold witness for Him because His Spirit lives in you.

Father God, equip me with boldness and wisdom to be an effective witness for You. I pray that You teach me how to present Your Son in a relevant way to those around me. Help me to never underestimate the power of sharing my testimony and just showing someone Your love by offering to pray for them. Father, thank You for sending Yeshua to die for me and for giving me Your Spirit so I can walk in power and be Your witness.

He Holds Your Hand

The steps of a man are established by the LORD, and He delights in his way. When he falls, he will not be hurled headlong, because the LORD is the One who holds his hand.

—PSALM 37:23–24

THINK ABOUT THIS: when you fall, you will get up again because the Lord holds your hand. I love this verse. Notice also that it says the Father delights in us. And when we stumble, we're not going to fall headlong because HaShem, the God of glory, is upholding us through Yeshua.

Doesn't that give you confidence and comfort? For me, there is truly no assurance in life other than the Lord. How could we possibly face death, aging, disease, or an unstable economy if our hope was solely in ourselves? Our only confidence and comfort is El Shaddai (God Almighty Himself).

I am sure that many of you feel like I do: that outside of God's love, the world feels like a scary place. How could anybody not be afraid when there is so much that we are not in control of? But when we know God as Father, we trust Him and are confident He will protect us.

Consider this: God is not only almighty and all-powerful; *He's also the most sensitive Being in the universe.* It's because of His tenderness toward us that He holds our hands and keeps us. When you falter, you're going to get back up, arise, and conquer because Yahweh is holding you.

We've heard the saying, "You can't keep a good man down." But the truth is not that you can't keep a good man down but rather, "You can't keep Yahweh down," and we have Yahweh. Baruch HaShem. Praise God!

> *Father God, I look to You today because I know those who hope in You will not be disappointed. You uphold me by Your mighty right hand, and Your Word declares that I can dwell under the shelter of Your wings. Father, give me a greater confidence in Your love for me. I pray for a greater assurance that You are with me and that You will never let me fall. Father, cause this truth to be planted deep in my heart so that I will arise like an eagle. In Messiah Yeshua's name.*

Seek Wisdom and Understanding

> Who among you is wise and understanding? Let him show by his good behavior his deeds in the gentleness of wisdom.
>
> —JAMES 3:13

WISDOM AND UNDERSTANDING release our ability to forgive.

Forgiveness is extremely important for walking in the Spirit. Jesus said, "If you forgive others for their transgressions, your heavenly Father will also forgive you. But if you do not forgive others, then your Father will not forgive your transgressions" (Matt. 6:14–15). When Jesus gave us the Lord's Prayer, He said we should ask the Father to "forgive us our debts, as we also have forgiven our debtors" (Matt. 6:12). This is how important forgiveness is to God. But how do we acquire the ability to forgive? Once again, through wisdom and understanding.

When Jesus was on the cross about to give up His life, He said, "Father, forgive them; for they do not know what they are doing" (Luke 23:34). In other words, Jesus had compassion on them because He had the understanding to see that those who mocked Him, plucked out His beard, and crucified Him didn't know what they were doing. They were in darkness and without understanding.

Often when people do things that offend us, they do those things because they are afraid and insecure. When we have wisdom, we will be able to see that. And when we see that, we will be able to have compassion on them just as Jesus had compassion on those who crucified Him. We will be able to see their need and have mercy. The Spirit's wisdom and understanding will free us to show them the love of God. This will not only please the Lord; it will allow us to have peace and to overcome. Beloved, I encourage you to ask God for wisdom today, because those who attain it obtain victory.

> *Father God, crown me today with Your mind. Give me the gift of wisdom, even as You gave Solomon wisdom. Father, in Yeshua's name, I ask that You also give me understanding so I can see beyond what people say and do, discern what is really motivating them, and respond to them with love, compassion, and forgiveness.*

True Riches

> Make sure that your character is free from the love of money, being content with what you have; for He Himself has said, "I will never desert you, nor will I ever forsake you."
>
> —HEBREWS 13:5

TODAY'S VERSE PRESENTS a godly perspective of what being rich really means. It's telling us that a rich person is not someone who has everything he wants but rather someone who has learned how to be content with what he has. The apostle Paul learned a secret about life—be at peace in every situation. He said, "I know how to get along with humble means, and I also know how to live in prosperity; in any and every circumstance I have learned the secret of being filled and going hungry, both of having abundance and suffering need" (Phil. 4:12).

One thing I've discovered is that the only people who think money is the answer are those who don't have money. It's the same with fame. The people who think fame would make them happy are those who have never had fame, because people who have been famous, including myself, know that fame doesn't satisfy. Likewise, those who have money know money isn't the answer. Now, I know that if we don't have enough money to put a roof over our heads and food in our stomachs and take care of real needs, we have some extremely significant challenges. But the point I am making is that the things we often think are the answer for our happiness are not. Paul was not chasing after things that could not satisfy him. He learned how to be content with simply being at peace within himself through the Lord.

Let's not waste our energy searching after vain things that can never fully satisfy. The Lord is our fullness. The apostle Paul said that "the kingdom of God is not eating and drinking, but righteousness and peace and joy in the Holy Spirit" (Rom. 14:17). Let's search for the One who will spring up from within us to become a well of living water so that we will thirst no more (John 4:14). In Messiah Jesus are all the treasures of life. In Him "are hidden all the treasures of wisdom and knowledge" (Col. 2:3). He has more for us than we imagine. All we need to do is give our whole heart to Him.

> *Father God, only You can truly satisfy. Fill me afresh with Your Holy Spirit. Let me drink from the rivers of Your living water so that I can truly find satisfaction. To God be the glory.*

Created in His Image

For since the creation of the world His invisible attributes, His eternal power and divine nature, have been clearly seen, being understood through what has been made, so that they are without excuse.

—ROMANS 1:20

GOD'S PRESENCE IS manifest through the beauty of His creation. When it comes to acknowledging and worshipping God, the Scriptures tell us that everyone is without excuse because God's invisible attributes such as His power, eternality, and glory are clearly seen in what He has made.

Imagine you are in a lush forest filled with gorgeous pine trees. You're surrounded by rivers and streams on every side, and there is a beautiful blue sky above with the sun shining down. I was in just such a surrounding not long ago in Colorado. The setting was so beautiful, it almost took my breath away. Now think about this: The same God who created that beautiful scene in Colorado also created you in His own image. In other words, the beauty we can clearly see in God's creation is in you and me, because the One who created all this beauty made us in His own image.

Beloved, you are beautiful to God. You and I are so much more valuable to the Father than we can comprehend. The beauty in us is vastly more incredible than the most gorgeous sites in nature. "I pray that the eyes of your heart may be enlightened, so that you will know what is the hope of His calling, what are the riches of the glory of His inheritance in the saints" (Eph. 1:18).

I want to encourage you today to believe you're beautiful. Know that God loves you. Because of the blood of Yeshua, you are accepted in His beloved Son and are not under condemnation. Your sin is being removed, and God's love is being poured out upon you. Now He wants your heart to rise back to Him and love Him in return.

> *Father God, open my mind and heart today to really believe that I am beautiful to You, that You love me, and that I am valuable to You. Thank You for pouring Your love out on me. I ask that You help me to consistently choose to love You in return.*

Choose Love

No one has seen God at any time; if we love one another, God abides in us, and His love is perfected in us.

—1 John 4:12

WE DON'T WALK by sight. We walk by the Spirit, and we can't see the Spirit on this side of glory. But if instead of trying to see the Spirit, we choose to know Messiah Jesus by walking in love, the apostle John tells us that we will be abiding in God Himself.

As a young believer, I didn't think much about love. I thought about climbing mountains and fighting. I thought about spiritual warfare. I thought about conquering. All of that is really important, but as I've matured I've come to understand that those who have truly grown strong and have deep roots in their relationship with God are walking in love.

Love is the greatest power of all. It is not first a feeling; it is a choice. God didn't say, "Whosoever feels…"; He said, "Whosoever will…." You see, the thing that makes you and me unique as human beings is that we have a conscious and free choice. All day long we're making choices. Animals don't have this freedom of choice. They don't have moral conscious awareness; they don't think through and process moral decisions. They just live by their survival instincts. But as human beings uniquely created in the image of God, we have consciousness and the power of choice. And the way we overcome is by choosing to walk in love.

Walking in love takes effort, that's for sure. It's like swimming upstream. But hear this: to really know Messiah Jesus, we must daily choose love. Like Yeshua, who so loved you and me that He gave His life for us, we must recognize that love involves putting others first and sacrificing for them. So whether it's through our thoughts, our actions, or our words, if we choose to walk in love each day, we'll know our Creator in a deeper way and come more fully into His light.

Father God, may the words of my mouth and the meditations of my heart be acceptable in Your sight. Make me conscious of whether my words, thoughts, and actions reflect Your love. Lord, You love me unconditionally. Help me to love others the way You love me.

Guard Against Deception

Let no one say when he is tempted, "I am being tempted by God"; for God cannot be tempted by evil, and He Himself does not tempt anyone.

—JAMES 1:13

MANY TIMES PEOPLE do things that are wrong, but they don't think they're wrong because they believe God is the One leading them. For instance, I've known too many people who have left their churches or even their marriage partners, claiming God told them to leave, when in reality, although they thought He said that, He didn't. People are doing things they think are OK with God but that, in fact, are not right. James is warning us not to be deceived.

I want to stress the truth in today's verse. Often when we love God and are sincerely seeking Him, we can make the mistake of thinking that everything we feel is from Him. We think all the thoughts we're thinking and all the emotions we're feeling are from the Lord when sometimes they're not.

This was a huge lesson I had to learn years ago. I knew

that God supernaturally spoke to me, but in my inexperience I made the mistake of thinking that every time I sensed something, it was the Lord. I had to learn the lesson found in 1 John 4:1–3, which says to test the spirits because not every spirit is from God.

The Bible says Satan disguises himself as an angel of light (2 Cor. 11:14). How, then, do we know what's from HaShem and what's not? First, we have the Word. If a thought, a feeling, a statement, or an action contradicts the written Word, it's not from the Lord. Second, the Scriptures tell us we gain discernment through experience and maturity. Hebrews 5:14 reveals to us that as our senses are trained by the Lord we are able "to discern good and evil." And third, counsel from mature and trusted friends in Messiah serves as a safeguard to keep us on track.

Beloved, I want to encourage us today: let's be on guard against deception and the pride Satan can use to deceive us.

> *Father God, I ask You to give me a discerning heart so I will know which thoughts and feelings are from You, which ones are from the enemy, and which ones are from my flesh. Father, give me deeper insight so I can test the spirits and know which impulse and voice to follow.*

No Condemnation

Therefore there is now no condemnation for those
who are in Christ Jesus.

—ROMANS 8:1

THIS IS AN incredible reality—you and I can be
assured that we are loved, forgiven, and accepted by
God. Every second, every hour, every day, you and I are
being embraced by the Father's love. There is no condemnation from the Father toward us. In order for us to
enter into a fuller dimension of this reality, we have to
be very careful to guard our hearts to ensure that we do
not condemn other people, because when we condemn
others, we open a door in our lives for the devil to put
thoughts of self-condemnation upon us.

This is why Jesus said, "Do not judge so that you
will not be judged. For in the way you judge, you will
be judged; and by your standard of measure, it will be
measured to you" (Matt. 7:1–2). He said something similar about forgiveness, telling us that if we forgive others,
our heavenly Father will also forgive us (Matt. 6:14).

Father's grace is extended toward us, so there is no

accusation. But in order to experience the fullness of this reality, we need to be very careful not to speak critically of others. And beyond our words, we need to guard against thoughts of condemnation, bitterness, ill will, and judgment. I know this is hard to do. We're in a battle, and Satan is an accuser.

In my own life, I try to watch my attitude and thoughts about people because I know that if I allow myself to have ill will toward somebody, I'm hurting myself. And worse than that, I'm in agreement with an evil spirit and not fulfilling God's call on my life. So, beloved, let's pay attention to our thoughts and not allow ourselves to accuse or condemn others. Let's keep our eyes on Jesus and walk in love. As we do, we will experience freedom from accusation ourselves.

> *Father God, You have forgiven me, and I ask You to help me forgive others. Father, help me to guard my heart and mind to resist the thoughts of the devil, thoughts of accusation and condemnation. Father, I purpose instead to have thoughts of good will, grace, and love toward others, even as You have shown me love.*

The Principle of the Sabbath

Remember the sabbath day, to keep it holy.
—EXODUS 20:8

OFTEN WHEN WE hear the word Sabbath, we think of the Ten Commandments given to Moses, of which the command to observe the Sabbath is the fourth. But the truth is that the Sabbath (Hebrew: Shabbat) is a principle of creation and actually predates the Law and the Hebrew people. Before the nation of Israel was born or the Ten Commandments were given, Genesis 2 says: "By the seventh day God completed His work which He had done, and He rested on the seventh day from all His work which He had done. Then God blessed the seventh day and *sanctified it*, because in it He rested from all His work which God had created and made" (vv. 2–3).

The word *sanctified* in verse 3 comes from the Hebrew word *kadosh*, which means holy, consecrated, separate, or set apart. From this principle we learn the importance of having time in our life that is separated unto God.

Taking a day each week to rest and be "human beings" rather than "human doings" creates a healthy boundary in our lives that will help us in our walk with God. This is why Yeshua said in Mark 2:27, "The Sabbath was made for man." To unplug from work, computers, cell phones, entertainment, or any other daily routines that contribute to stress is something we must discipline ourselves to practice. I am so busy during the week that I literally have to force myself to take a day of rest. But I am able to function in greater health because of it.

Beloved, don't dismiss the importance of taking a day each week to spend quality time with and unto God. It is not a day of recreation but a day of sanctification. Shabbat is about the Lord. We honor Him by setting it apart unto Him. In return, He brings us into a deeper place of healing, peace, and fellowship with Him. We imitate our God, who Himself rested on the seventh day, and as a result of following His example, we will be blessed and refreshed.

> *Father God, thank You for giving me a pattern to follow by working six days and resting one when You created the heavens and the earth. Help me to prioritize taking a day to honor You and disconnect from work, busyness, and stress in order to be refreshed and restored. Thank You for the Sabbath.*

Don't Rely on the Flesh

The LORD will fight for you while you keep silent.
—EXODUS 14:14

THIS VERSE REMINDS me that there is a time to simply hold our peace and see God go to work on our behalf. This is particularly true when it comes to responding to our enemies. Oftentimes the Lord is telling us to just turn the other cheek and let Him fight the battle for us.

Now, there is a time to stand up for yourself, and only the Holy Spirit can instruct you when you should and shouldn't act or speak. But one of the things we have to master is holding our peace so God can go before us. You see, if we're always taking matters into our own hands, we'll never see God act. Sometimes in order to see God act, we have to stop acting.

There was a time in my life when I said to myself, "I'm never going to know for sure if God is the one opening these doors or if I'm the one doing this unless I stop." So I did nothing for a year but simply wait on God. At the end of that year I saw God supernaturally open doors for me that I could never in a thousand years have opened for myself.

I want to encourage you, beloved, not to rely on the weapons of your flesh. Don't take matters into your own hands. Messiah Yeshua said He did nothing by His own initiative; He did only what He saw the Father doing (John 5:19–20). So let's stop acting in the flesh and stand still to see the salvation of the Lord. The Bible says those that wait upon Him will rise up with wings like eagles (Isa. 40:31).

Now, on the other hand, if you have a spirit of passivity, God may be calling you to take initiative. But for many believers, it's not a spirit of passivity that's their problem; it's that they're trying to manipulate things in their own strength. If that's you, God is saying, "Just stand still and watch Me fight on your behalf."

> *Father God, like Yeshua, I want to do only what I see You doing. Father, give me the discernment to know when to be still and when to act. I don't want to take matters into my own hands or rely on my flesh. Help me to fully rely on You and see You bring me victory.*

Come Together

And let us consider how to stimulate one another to love and good deeds, not forsaking our own assembling together, as is the habit of some, but encouraging one another; and all the more as you see the day drawing near.

—HEBREWS 10:24–25

I REALIZE THAT SOME people for health and other reasons are not able to physically attend or be part of local congregations. I bless them, and I thank God for Christian television, live streaming, and other means available today that allow us to encourage, teach, and share the gospel with those who can't leave home. But this verse is stressing the importance of assembling together with God's people. It is vital that we fellowship with other believers.

Thanks to social media and various technology, this can be done even when people are not physically together. There are apps such as YouVersion that allow people to share prayer requests, and some churches offer online small groups. It is a rich experience to be physically assembled with other believers who love the Lord, but when that is not possible, the phone and other technology give us a way to stay connected with God's people to study the Word together, share prayer needs, and talk about the things of the kingdom.

As the day of the Lord draws near and things on planet Earth get more difficult, we are going to need to be connected so we can keep one another encouraged in our faith. So be intentional about staying joined to and united with the body. I want to encourage you according to today's verse to fellowship with other believers on a regular basis. This is important to Yeshua as well as for your own growth. Jesus said where two or three are gathered in His name, He is there in the midst of them (Matt. 18:20). That means there is an anointing that comes only when we're in a corporate environment. So let's gather together with God's people on a regular basis to honor Yeshua, stay encouraged, grow, and be a blessing.

Father God, help me to make it a priority to fellowship with and stay connected to Your body.

The Lord Is With You

With Your counsel You will guide me, and afterward receive me to glory.

—Psalm 73:24

READ TODAY'S VERSE again. The psalmist declared by faith that God was with him in the present, was going to keep him and guide him in the future, and in the end would receive him into glory. I love this verse. It contains the essence of what a confident and intimate relationship with God looks like.

Asaph, the psalmist here, knew that when he died, he was going to go straight into the glory of His Father. It's just as Yeshua said: "In My Father's house are many mansions; if it were not so, I would have told you. I go to prepare a place for you" (John 14:2, NKJV). Beloved, Yeshua has prepared a place for you and me.

What a carefree life we would have if we knew and believed in the innermost part of our being that God is with us—He's closer to us than our own heartbeat—and that as we move forward in life, He's going to guide us, and at the end of our days, we will join Yeshua in paradise.

In Isaiah 41:10 the Lord tells us, "Do not fear, for I am with you; do not anxiously look about you, for I am your God. I will strengthen you, surely I will help you, surely I will uphold you with My righteous right hand." The same truth is echoed in Deuteronomy 31:6, Joshua 1:9, Zephaniah 3:17, and many other scriptures because our God wants us to receive it.

Beloved, if we would really take hold of this truth, we would live in joy, confidence, and peace. Today, I release and speak a word of faith over your life to go forward with confidence in the name of Messiah Jesus, knowing your God is with you, will lead you in the future, and has a place prepared for you in His glory.

Father God, I ask You to steel me and give me sureness and backbone in my confidence in You. Gird me in the foundation of Your Son by Your Spirit. Yeshua, cause Your truth to be planted deep in my heart. You are my guide and my confidence. I trust in You.

Speak Words That Bring Life

When there are many words, transgression is unavoidable, but he who restrains his lips is wise.

—PROVERBS 10:19

IF WE'RE NOT careful we can easily forget that just as God spoke the heavens and earth into existence, so too every word that comes out of our mouths is a spiritual act of creation. When we speak words of hatred, criticism, judgment, or gossip, those words do not just die; they affect both individuals and the spiritual atmosphere surrounding our lives. Likewise, when we exhort others with love, honor, affirmation, or inspiration, these words too continue to have power. Our words are not inconsequential. With the same mouth we can speak encouragement, giving life, or discouragement, causing "death."

Jesus said in Mark 7:15, "There is nothing outside the man which can defile him if it goes into him; but the things which proceed out of the man are what defile the man." We may think we are disciples of Jesus because we have some of the outer things right—we attend church; we pray; we read our Bibles. But if our words are not full of life and the Holy Spirit, then we are deceiving ourselves. It takes discipline to control our words when someone does something that frustrates, irritates, or angers us. It takes willpower to control our tongues. But remember, our words can defile and divide, or they can build up and bring life. This is a big and far-reaching reality to ponder.

Proverbs 4:23 says, "Watch over your heart with all diligence, for from it flow the springs of life." The day is coming when each of us will stand before the throne and give an account of every word we have spoken (2 Cor. 5:10; Rom. 14:10). If we are going to live victoriously in Jesus, we need to be mindful of the words we speak. So I encourage you today, beloved one, submit your tongue to God and guard your heart and your words.

> *Father God, I repent right now for every word I have spoken carelessly, for every time I spoke death instead of life. I am sorry for those times when my words were filled with judgment, accusation, and spite. Please forgive me. I cannot take back what I have said, but I declare that from this day forward, I will submit my tongue to You. By Your grace and Your Spirit, Father, help me to guard my heart and my words. I will use my mouth to speak life and glorify You, in Yeshua's name.*

Share Your Faith

Who has believed our message? And to whom has
the arm of the LORD been revealed?

—ISAIAH 53:1

HAVE YOU EVER wondered why there are so few
Jewish believers in Jesus in the world? Isaiah prophesied this would happen 2,700 years ago. In today's verse,
he prophesied that when the Messiah appeared in Israel,
not many of God's first covenant people, the Jews, would
believe in Him.

We read how this prophecy was fulfilled in the Gospel
of John, which states that Yeshua "came to His own [the
Jewish people], and those who were His own did not
receive Him" (John 1:11). In other words, during Jesus'
first coming, most of the nation of Israel has been blind
to who Yeshua is. Paul talks about this in Romans 11
when he writes that a temporary hardness or a blindness
has come upon Israel until the fullness of the Gentiles
has come in.

But as we move closer to the end of the age, God is
going to open the eyes of a critical mass of Jewish people

to recognize who Jesus is. The good news for Gentile believers is that God is going to use many of you to do that. And when there is a mass of Jewish people who have come to faith in Jesus, crying out, "Blessed is He who comes in the name of the Lord" (Matt. 23:39), this will usher in Yeshua's return.

Of course, it isn't always easy to share your faith with Jewish people. Some may become angry or offended, but we must be more concerned about obeying Jesus than being liked. The Jewish people have suffered years of persecution, so you must come to them humbly; you may even be led to apologize for anti-Semitism they may have suffered. But as you share how Jesus fulfilled the Messianic prophecies (in Isaiah 53, for example) and tell them what He has done in your life, you will be planting a seed God can use to draw them to Himself.

Romans 11:15 says that as Jewish people come to faith in Messiah Yeshua, the church will experience such revival, it will be like "life from the dead."

Father God, I ask for courage to share Your love with the Jewish people I come in contact with and for wisdom to know what to say and when. Give me Your heart for Israel and for their salvation.

He Validates You

Just as He chose us in Him before the foundation of the world, that we would be holy and blameless before Him. In love....In Him we have redemption through His blood, the forgiveness of our trespasses, according to the riches of His grace.

—EPHESIANS 1:4, 7

WHEN JESUS GAVE His life on the cross, He did not do it just to forgive our sins, as important as that is. Even beyond that, He did it to purchase us for Himself. We are His inheritance. We are what He gave His life for. It is because of us that He took the nails in His hands, the spear in His side, and the nails in His feet. He did it to redeem us, to buy us. We are valued and treasured by the Lord, our Father God, way, way beyond what we currently comprehend. This is why Paul prayed for us in Ephesians 1:18 that we would know "what are the riches of the glory of His inheritance in the saints."

I want you to realize how essential you are to God's heart. You are truly esteemed by your Father. You are special and important beyond any words that I could use. He chose you for Himself. Again, I pray with Paul "that the eyes of your heart may be enlightened, so that you will know what is the hope of His calling, what are the riches of the glory of His inheritance in the saints" (Eph. 1:18). That means in you!

In fact, you are so embraced by God, you are called the bride of Christ (Rev. 19:7)! Beloved, your importance, your value, and your significance are so much greater than any validation this world or any person on earth could ever give you. But if we are depending on the world to tell us how treasured we are, if we are depending on someone to validate us, we are going to be disappointed.

Neither the world nor anybody in it can ever affirm us in a way that measures how valuable we truly are to the Father. The Father's love for us is demonstrated by the fact that He sacrificed His Son so that we would become His inheritance. That is the ultimate act of validation. We are destined to be married to the One who chose us when we see Him face to face at the marriage supper of the Lamb (Rev. 19:9). We will be cherished forever.

> *Father God, help me to receive the truth of Your love for me in the deep places of my heart. Thank You for making me significant. Help me to never look to the world to validate me.*

Walk in Love

There is one body and one Spirit, just as also you
were called in one hope of your calling; one Lord,
one faith, one baptism, one God and Father of all
who is over all and through all and in all.

—EPHESIANS 4:4–6

SADLY, THERE IS a lot of division among believers
today, and some of us don't even realize how important it is to God that we do as much as possible to be in
solidarity with the greater body of Christ. The older I get
in the Lord, the more I realize how much unity is part
of God's heart. In Jesus' last words in John 17, in what is
called the high priestly prayer, He prayed, "That they may
all be one; even as You, Father, are in Me and I in You,
that they also may be in Us, so that the world may believe
that You sent Me" (v. 21).

When we walk in dissension with other believers, it
grieves God's heart. I realize that sometimes unity is not
possible. Sometimes the other person won't let us be in
unity with them. But we should do everything we can
in the Spirit to be at peace and in solidarity. The apostle

Paul told us to avoid useless arguments that lead to nothing but dissension and to concentrate on the things we can do to build one another up (2 Tim. 2:20–26).

Sometimes people make doctrine overly divisive. One person believes the correct way to baptize is through immersion and another through sprinkling. Personally, I believe in baptizing by immersion, but if someone comes from a background where baptism was done by pouring or sprinkling, I'm not going to make an issue out of that and cause a separation in my relationship with that person. If the subject comes up, I'd be happy and blessed to share my view in love. But I'm not going to let that subject cause a break in the relationship.

I want to encourage you, beloved, to walk in unity. Walk in love. And when you do, you'll experience Jesus' presence in your life in a greater way because the Bible says God is love, and He that loves knows God (1 John 4:7–8).

Father God, train me to walk in unity with others. Help me to avoid foolish arguments and be quick to forgive. I understand that disunity grieves Your heart, so I ask You to give me the grace to live in peace with all Your children as much as possible (Rom. 12:8), even when it is difficult for me in the natural.

Trust Brings Peace

The steadfast of mind You will keep in perfect peace, because he trusts in You.

—Isaiah 26:3

IN A WAY, today's verse doesn't really make sense. Wouldn't a person with a steadfast mind already have peace? It's the next line that gives us insight: "because he trusts in You." In other words, one thing undergirds both the steadfast mind and the peace that Isaiah speaks of—trust. We will enjoy both these pillars when we truly trust HaShem.

But what does it mean to trust God? One thing it involves is clinging to Him. Many of us say we trust God, but the truth is that we're not really clinging to Him. We don't walk through life talking to Him on a daily basis. We don't communicate with Him constantly. We don't lift up all the things we're going through to Him. In short, we are not practically depending on Messiah.

We say we trust in Him, but we're compartmentalizing Him. We worry about our problems while claiming to believe He is all-powerful and can take care of all the things that concern us. In many ways, we are often like Martha in Luke 10. She was anxious about preparing food and being a good hostess when Jesus was literally sitting in her living room. She missed the main thing.

Her preoccupation with all of her tasks and concerns kept her from sitting at Yeshua's feet. Jesus told her, "Martha, Martha, you are worried and bothered about so many things; but only one thing is necessary" (Luke 10:41–42). That one thing is to cling to Him—to sit at His feet, worship, and bring our concerns constantly before Him.

Beloved, if we will walk in such a way that we're always cultivating a sense of His presence and lordship, sharing everything with Him and clinging to Him, we're going to become more steadfast and our souls will sink into a deeper peace.

> *Father God, I believe You are all-powerful and are able to address everything that concerns me and meet my every need. Help me to turn to You with my cares and concerns. I know I need to cling to You instead of relying on my own strength and manipulations. Father, bring me into a deeper reality of the experience of Your peace as I focus my mind and heart on You. Through Your grace, in my Messiah Yeshua's name.*

About the Author

MESSIANIC RABBI KIRT A. Schneider, a Jewish believer in Jesus and end-times messenger of the Lord, delivers the word of the Lord with a true passion of the Holy Spirit. When Rabbi Schneider was twenty years old, the Lord suddenly awakened him and revealed Himself as Jesus the Messiah, and his life has never been the same. He has since pastored, traveled internationally as an evangelist, served as rabbi of a Messianic synagogue, and is currently a *schliach* (messenger) of Jesus the Messiah to the world.

Rabbi Schneider is the host of the international television broadcast *Discovering the Jewish Jesus*, which can be seen seven days a week in more than one hundred million homes in the United States and approximately two hundred nations worldwide. Viewers tune in regularly as Rabbi Schneider shows with exceptional clarity how the Tanach (Old) and New Testaments connect like a hand in a glove. For a list of times and stations that broadcast Rabbi Schneider's program in your area, visit www.DiscoveringTheJewishJesus.com and click on the

"Ways to Watch" tab. His program can also be viewed via YouTube, Roku, and Facebook.

In addition to hosting mass evangelistic outreaches and broadcasting through television around the world, Rabbi Schneider is the author of several books, including *The Mystery of Dreams*, *Rivers of Revelation*, *The Lion of Judah*, *Experiencing the Supernatural*, *The Book of Revelation Decoded*, *Do Not Be Afraid!*, and *Awakening to Messiah*. He and his wife, Cynthia, have two children and have been married since 1983.

www.DiscoveringTheJewishJesus.com

DISCOVERING THE JEWISH JESUS

CONNECT WITH RABBI SCHNEIDER

www.DiscoveringTheJewishJesus.com

 www.facebook.com/rabbischneider

 @RabbiSchneider

 @discoveringthejewishjesus

 https://www.youtube.com/user/
RabbiSchneider